NO. 2 WINTER 1996

NEW DIRECTIONS FOR SCHOOL LEADERSHIP

Boundary Crossings

Educational Partnerships and School Leadership

RICHARD H. ACKERMAN

University of Massachusetts Lowell

Harvard Graduate School of Education

EDITOR-IN-CHIEF

PAULA A. CORDEIRO

University of Connecticut

EDITOR

BOUNDARY CROSSINGS: EDUCATIONAL PARTNERSHIPS AND SCHOOL LEADERSHIP
Paula Cordeiro (ed.)
New Directions for School Leadership, No. 2, Winter 1996
Richard H. Ackerman, Editor-in-Chief

Microfilm copies of issues and articles are available in 16 mm and 35 mm, as well as microfiche in 105 mm, through University Microfilms Inc., 300 North Zeeb Road, Ann Arbor, Michigan 48106–1346.

ISSN 1089–5612   ISBN 0–7879–9862–1

NEW DIRECTIONS FOR SCHOOL LEADERSHIP is part of The Jossey-Bass Education Series and is published quarterly by Jossey-Bass Inc., Publishers, 350 Sansome Street, San Francisco, California 94104–1342.

SUBSCRIPTIONS: Please see Ordering Information on p. iv.
EDITORIAL CORRESPONDENCE should be sent to Richard Ackerman, The Principals' Center, Harvard Graduate School of Education, 336 Gutman Library, Cambridge, MA, 02138.

 Manufactured in the United States of America on Lyons Falls Pathfinder Tradebook. This paper is acid-free and 100 percent totally chlorine-free.

The International Network of Principals' Centers

The International Network of Principals' Centers sponsors *New Directions for School Leadership* as part of its commitment to strengthening leadership at the individual school level through professional development for leaders. The Network has a membership of principals' centers, academics, and practitioners in the United States and overseas and is open to all groups and institutions committed to the growth of school leaders and the improvement of schools. The Network currently functions primarily as an information exchange and support system for member centers in their efforts to work directly with school leaders in their communities. Its office is in the Principals' Center at the Harvard Graduate School of Education.

The Network offers these services:

- The International Directory of Principals' Centers features member centers with contact persons, descriptions of center activities, program references, and evaluation instruments.
- The Annual Conversation takes place every spring, when members meet for seminars, workshops, speakers, and to initiate discussions that will continue throughout the year.
- *Newsnotes*, the Network's quarterly newsletter, informs members of programs, conferences, workshops, and special interest items.
- *Reflections*, an annual journal, includes articles by principals, staff developers, university educators, and principals' center staff members.

For further information, please contact:

International Network of Principals' Centers
Harvard Graduate School of Education
336 Gutman Library
Cambridge, MA 02138
(617) 495–9812

Ordering Information

NEW DIRECTIONS FOR SCHOOL LEADERSHIP
This series of paperback books provides principals, superintendents, teachers, and others who exercise leadership at the local level with insight and guidance on the important issues influencing schools and school leadership. Books in the series are published quarterly in Fall, Winter, Spring and Summer and are available for purchase both by subscription and individually.

SUBSCRIPTIONS for 1997–1998 cost $52.00 for individuals (a savings of 35 percent over single-copy prices) and $96.00 for libraries. There are no shipping and handling charges on subscriptions.

SINGLE COPIES cost $20.00 plus shipping. There will be handling charges on billed orders. Call the 800 number below for more information.

SINGLE COPIES AVAILABLE FOR SALE

SL1   Every Teacher as a Leader: Realizing the Potential of Teacher Leadership, *Gayle Moller, Marilyn Katzenmeyer*

SL2   Boundary Crossings: Educational Partnerships and School Leadership, *Paula A. Cordeiro*

QUANTITY DISCOUNTS ARE AVAILABLE. Please contact Jossey-Bass Periodicals for information at 1–415–433–1740.

TO ORDER, CALL 1–800–956–7739 or 1–415–433–1767
. . . and visit our website at http://www.josseybass.com

Contents

1. Introduction: Connecting school communities through
   educational partnerships   *1*
   Paula A. Cordeiro, Mary Monroe Kolek
   A discussion of the conditions necessary to create, support, and
   institutionalize successful partnerships between schools and
   community organizations.

2. Nurturing partnerships between schools and families   *15*
   Roy M. Seitsinger, Jr.
   It is essential that schools build partnerships with families. The author
   defines the role that local administrators play in achieving those kinds of
   close links, to move toward founding a caring community of learners.

3. Partnerships between schools and institutions of
   higher education   *31*
   L. Nan Restine
   There are both possibilities and problems in developing meaningful
   partnerships between schools and institutions of higher learning.

4. Strategies for fostering partnerships between educators and
   health and human services professionals   *41*
   Ellen Smith Sloan
   Data from a case study describe a partnership between educators and
   school-based health center professionals and the leadership strategies
   a school principal used to ensure its success.

5. Using the arts to integrate knowledge: Partnerships between
   schools and nonprofit organizations   *57*
   Liane Brouillette
   A case study depicts a partnership with a nonprofit arts agency. The author
   discusses the problems that can be avoided when individuals from two different organizational cultures build a partnership.

6. The potential for partnerships between schools and religious
   organizations   *71*
   Richard D. Lakes, Paula A. Cordeiro
   The authors describe a number of programs offered to urban youth by
   church-related organizations and identify possible links to schools.

7. A university, business foundation, and school
   working together   *85*
   Betty Merchant

   There are special opportunities and concerns in creating a three-way
   partnership. The author offers recommendations for sustaining this
   kind of collaboration.

8. Understanding the organizational dynamics of collaborative
   partnerships: Two frameworks   *99*
   Bob L. Johnson, Jr., Patrick F. Galvin

   Two theoretical frameworks—public choice and organizational
   economics—may be used for analyzing the potential problems and
   benefits of forming educational partnerships.

9. The implications of partnerships for the preparation and professional growth of educational leaders   *115*
   Paula A. Cordeiro, Karen S. Loup

   The authors identify the overlapping themes of the previous chapters and
   offer ideas for improving the preparation of educational leaders.

Index   *127*

The authors describe the conditions necessary for schools to form and support partnerships with other organizations and agencies. They explain how these collaborations require educational leaders to be boundary crossers and compradors.

1

Introduction: Connecting school communities through educational partnerships

Paula A. Cordeiro, Mary Monroe Kolek

PARTNERING HAS BECOME THE BUZZWORD of the nineties. Although the concept once was primarily the province of the business community, partnerships and collaboration are now increasingly used as tools to stimulate and promote reforms within and between education, business, and human service agencies and organizations.

In education, partnerships are either school-linked or school-based. They range in complexity from one-on-one partnerships, with one school collaborating with a single person, organization, or agency, to multilayered alliances. Recent literature indicates that partnering is not only useful, it is quickly becoming mandatory in

For the purpose of writing this introduction we collected data from fourteen in-depth, elite interviews transcribed verbatim from audiotapes. Four participants held positions in public schools: two superintendents, a director of public relations, and a school-business-community coordinator. Nine held positions outside schools: a director of off-campus programs at a community technical college; two priests, one Episcopalian and one Catholic; a director of a county juvenile justice system; a state director of family resource centers; a director of youth services for an urban community; a regional director for the state Department of Children and Families; and two project directors for two regional education service centers.

NEW DIRECTIONS FOR SCHOOL LEADERSHIP, NO. 2, WINTER 1996 ©JOSSEY-BASS PUBLISHERS today's economic and social climate. The question many educators face is not *if* but *how* to evolve from demonstration projects and pilots to adopting partnerships as regular elements of their school's service delivery model.

This discussion responds to this question by briefly reviewing the current status of educational partnerships. We then examine, using an analysis of elite interviews conducted with a variety of leaders participating in educational partnerships, the principles, conditions, and characteristics that support effective collaborations. Finally, the concept of the *comprador*, a boundary-crossing ambassador who serves as the necessary link between multiple cultures, is introduced as a new ingredient essential to establishing effective collaborations.

The changing role of educational partnerships

Since the days of the common school, public schools have formed partnerships with a variety of organizations. Unlike true partnerships, which by definition entail reciprocity between partners who enjoy similar benefits, these early relationships were usually of a more charitable nature, formed to allow the outside partner to supply the school with a needed service or resource pro bono.

Since the 1960s, several factors have coalesced to broaden the benefits to schools of long-term collaborations with organizations and agencies outside education. For example, the expansion of the educational system to include all children, including children with special needs, has made partnership benefits more practical. Also, the number of years children are in school has expanded. In many districts there are now programs to address children's needs from birth until age twenty-one. This has resulted in partnerships with families; the medical, social service, and business communities; and myriad other community agencies.

Another factor that has had a significant impact on collaborative efforts in education is the increase in the heterogeneity of the nation's population. This is reflected in the manner in which Americans live. Compared with thirty years ago, today's families are much more diverse. There are fewer "nuclear" families (a sole breadwinner, a full-time homemaker, plus children) and more families with stepchildren, dual-earner families, nontraditional households (composed of people not related by blood), and single-parent families (Outtz, 1993). As Americans have become increasingly transient, they have lost the informal networks of family and friends that traditionally provided children and families with an array of services and resources. The public schools remain the only system connecting the majority of citizens, and out of necessity they have assumed the support role previously supplied by people's friends and extended families (Lerner, 1995).

A framework for thinking about partnerships

In their book *The Teamnet Factor,* Lipnack and Stamps (1995) describe five elements that are fundamental to successful business partnerships and collaborative efforts:

- A unifying purpose
- A critical number of committed independent members
- Voluntary links that form a web of relationships
- Participants who assume specific responsibilities and function as multiple leaders
- Connections at many interactive levels in the environment

These elements have great significance for educational partnerships. Respondents identified all five as key contributors to the effectiveness of such partnerships. Although in reality these elements are synergistic, each is considered separately below for the purpose of studying and understanding them.

A common purpose

The unifying purpose that prompts schools, people, and organizations to collaborate in educational partnerships is best depicted by the now much quoted African proverb "It takes an entire village to raise a child." These partnerships form because individuals from disparate businesses and government agencies want to address the academic, social, emotional, physical, and ethical development of their community's children. This common imperative is the unifying purpose for any educational partnership with an outside agency or organization. Partners frequently describe a key moment when they realized that by acting together they could more effectively address one or more of the essential factors in the development of children. As one participant in our study commented, "a lot of our children come to us with economic and social problems that affect the way they learn; so we need all kinds of resources to help us with our job."

Autonomy

A second necessary element described by Lipnack and Stamps is the independence of partnership members. They argue against the assertion that joining a network forces a person to give up his or her independence. As the chapters in this sourcebook detail, people involved in partnerships are constantly stepping into the other partners' territory. This crossing of boundaries may be physical, although with today's technology it is increasingly accomplished via a variety of mediums. No matter what the means, when independent partners from different organizations come together, they enter one another's cybernetic work spaces. Like world travelers, partners do not give up their native citizenship, but they are expected to live and work within the culture they are "visiting" and working within. Collaboration among independent partners results in a synergistic relationship, one with processes and products that are richer than those that come from each person or agency working alone.

One study participant with the job title "coordinator of school-business-community partnerships" commented, "If I bring a program to the school . . . there's no way I can force it on my district. I have to go through channels, and it really ends up with the teacher. . . . It's not until that point, until the teachers say we like it, we want to try it, that you have something to start with."

Voluntary links to and from the schoolhouse

Partnerships are by definition voluntary in nature. Two or more independent agents agree to work together to accomplish a common purpose that is mutually beneficial. Each person interviewed for our study noted that trust is the essential element that forges and sustains voluntary relationships.

Boundary crossing and voluntary connections will not occur unless opportunities for relationships to grow are planned for and provided by the school. One respondent, a school-business community coordinator, discussed the importance of partners' developing trust over time: "It takes quite a bit of time. . . . It's almost like a person has to build up a level of trust so people feel they want to be involved with the project."

These relationships are forged through both physical and technological interactions. Easy access to telephones, computers with electronic mail, and fax machines is a minimum requirement necessary to shatter the walls of isolation surrounding the teacher in the classroom.

Emergent leaders

Traditionally, school districts have had a superintendent at the top of the hierarchy, with central office staff next in line, followed by the principal and assistant principal. There may then be a department chair or team leader, with the remainder of the staff situated at the bottom of the pyramid. Unfortunately, this organizational chart will probably change little in the next few decades. However, the spaces between the levels will nearly disappear in those schools and districts that restructure themselves into true learning communities by forming multiple partnerships.

In organizations and partnerships with a flattened hierarchy, leadership is no longer the exclusive domain of those positions with line authority. Instead, leadership emerges depending on the situation and needs of each participant. When people from different organizations and agencies collaborate with educators, leadership becomes a part of each participant's role.

Leadership needs and structures vary depending on the stage of development, size, and complexity of the partnership. In discussing her recently created position, a school-business-community coordinator commented, " I report to the superintendent. . . . I also report to the school-business-community partnership board of directors . . . who hold the purse strings. . . . There are certain people on that committee who are designated to be there, to sit down with me to make the decision as to where the monies go. . . . You have a combination of school and business people on that committee."

A web of relationships

The fifth element described by Lipnack and Stamps as fundamental to successful partnership efforts deals with patterns of interaction within the partnership. As stated earlier, school districts are hierarchical networks. As teachers, administrators, and support personnel in partnerships are required to cross boundaries, they will begin to see outside the layers of their own system.

We learn to view our world in the same way that it is constructed. Traditionally, educators did not need to view the world in more than one dimension. However, recent reforms in education, including the increase in the number of educational partnerships, requires a new vision, one with multiple perspectives and one that views complexity in a new way.

In *The Fifth Discipline*, Peter Senge (1990) differentiates between "detailed complexity" and "dynamic complexity." Detailed complexity is linear, allowing, if one is sufficiently determined, for the identification of all the possible variables that could influence a particular problem. Dynamic complexity is multidimensional, recognizing that multiple factors, over time, interact to create situations that cannot be understood or appreciated if viewed from only one perspective. Like the currently popular "magic eye" art that rewards viewers who can retrain their eyes to see multiple dimensions, partnerships will retrain participants to see outside the layers of the system. A web of connections will emerge as partners readjust their vision to meet the demands of boundary crossing.

As described by the participants in our study, once a glimmer of the possibilities is experienced, school personnel (and students) take on the roles of liaisons connecting people, organizations, and agencies. Those participating in successful collaborations indicate that the rewards for this new way of seeing are as surprising and addictive as the magic eye.

Once one has experienced this new way of seeing, problems no longer appear linear, with a single cause, effect, and solution. Instead, one sees a problem as a series of intersecting events and resources, all providing opportunities for intervention and instruction. The implications for education can be seen in the following examples of programming for school dropouts.

There are myriad recognized factors that correlate with children dropping out of school: absenteeism and tardiness, elementary grade retention, working more than fifteen hours per week, peer pressure, lack of involvement in extracurricular activities, and low socioeconomic status, to name but a few. And yet, despite educators' knowledge about these factors, in most cases interventions do not produce expected outcomes.

In this volume, we propose that this type of failure is due to the fact that most interventions are designed using a linear, one-dimensional model of problem solving and are narrowly targeted, usually at the point when the problem (dropping out) occurs. In reality, the problem is dynamic and complex, with multiple points of origin and thus multiple opportunities for intervention.

The decision to drop out of school usually results from an accumulation of dynamic, complex circumstances that occur and interact over time. Because "cause and effect are distant from each other in complex systems and therefore difficult to trace" (Stacey, 1992 p. 78)—if indeed they are traceable—it is impossible to design a single-point-in-time solution that is highly effective.

Focusing dropout prevention programs on middle or high schools is analogous to a surgeon's implanting an artificial heart—a solution that, no matter how technologically advanced, is narrowly focused and intervenes at the end of the problem instead of at the beginning stages, when multiple opportunities for prevention exists. It is much better—and more cost-effective—to change the patient's eating and exercise habits before heart disease develops. Similarly, instead of relying on narrowly focused interventions targeted at adolescents, communities can, through collaborative efforts, proactively address the problem of dropouts beginning with very young children. Head Start, Birth-to-Three, and Reading Recovery are but a few examples of early, multiple-alliance interventions designed to reduce the likelihood of children's dropping out of school.

Helping institutions and caring relationships protect children and nurture their resiliency. Youth and social service agencies, religious and ethnic associations, schools, and families are all partners in prevention, intervention, and treatment services. These partnerships are comparable to the good dietary habits and regular physical exercise necessary for healthy, disease-free bodies. They provide a safety net for children, reducing the need for more intrusive "intensive care" later in life.

Building on the framework: creating successful partnerships

Having examined the critical elements of effective partnerships, we now move to a consideration of the processes of developing, sustaining, and enhancing collaborations. Here we discuss characteristics of effective partnerships and the conditions that promote, maintain, and institutionalize them.

Conditions precedent

Respondents in our study identified five key factors as preconditions for successful partnerships: leadership, trust, stability, readiness, and a common agenda. A major theme that emerged in the interviews was the notion that within an organization a single person conceptualizes the original idea for the partnership. Several interviewees described the formation of at least the original partnership as "serendipitous," a fortuitous moment when the realization occurred that an unfulfilled need matched a resource that had previously crossed the partners' path. A partnership was then born from the partners' recognizing the opportunity and being willing to take a risk and step into one another's territory. Describing the formation of a partnership among three school districts and a local museum, a regional service center project director summarized the efforts of one of the school superintendents: "He saw this great resource sitting in his community, and the schools weren't using the expertise there. So, he talked with other people within the district and nearby districts, and the idea was developed further."

One clergyman, when referring to a partnership between his church and a local elementary school, commented on the role played by the school principal: "She was the one who . . . helped it grow. . . . It's her openness to the community. . . . It's person-to-person click. . . . She's providing the spark." All of the partnerships discussed by those interviewed had in common the *leadership* of one person who shared an idea with others in order to carry it out.

The second factor participants reported as a necessary prerequisite to establishing a partnership was *trust*. Before entering a partnership, participants must understand that the cultures of organizations differ. The school principal quoted above would not have taken her idea to the local church unless there already existed a relationship of trust.

A third critical precondition is *stability*. In discussing a meeting called by a communitywide group formed to address youth violence, one of the priests commented, "It's been terrible working with them. We don't know each other. I see the people heading that [program] as absolutely [temporary]. They don't know the community. . . . Nobody knew where anybody else was coming from. We didn't have the time—or the interest, frankly." Potential partners who discover a lack of long-term commitment on the part of fellow participants ask themselves the same questions as the clergyman: "Why should I spend my time on this issue when these people won't be here in the future? They aren't connected to this community, they haven't taken the time to establish a common agenda."

Another condition precedent to forming a successful partnership is *readiness*. Several of those interviewed described the importance of "tilling the soil." This prework included making and nurturing connections, constantly scanning the environment for opportunities that match identified needs, waiting for the time to be right politically, and planting seeds in several "fields."

A final factor considered to be important by many respondents was the need to define a *common agenda* (using a common language). The director of a grant-writing agency saw this step as absolutely essential. She noted that potential partners carry with them assumptions and perspectives that are likely to have meanings unique to their own organization's culture, even when described using the same language. Once an agenda is identified, however, partners have a common ground and can work more effectively to overcome obstacles.

Conditions that support partnerships

Respondents identified four additional factors or conditions that support collaboration. A key factor, mentioned by nearly all the participants, was good *communication*. As respondents discussed the swampy problems they dealt with, they repeatedly mentioned the need for organizational structures or strategies that enhance communication. An essential element of good communication is easy interfacing. Face-to-face communication using a common language was cited as the most effective means of building partnerships and solving problems. The use of technology, be it telephones, faxes, or electronic mail, was identified as a means of maintaining personal links and streamlining efforts to share information.

A second factor important in maintaining established partnerships is *reciprocity*. One participant commented, "You have to always remember, no matter what side of the fence you're working with, whether it's the school group or the community group . . . people want to know what's in it for them . . . how they fit into the picture. You ask them to tell you what kinds of things they would like to get out of this partnership." Another participant commented, "Everyone needs to get something out of the collaboration."

A third condition found to be crucial for sustaining a collaboration was *alignment and/or pooling of resources*. One participant explained, "We don't want to duplicate services that . . . already [exist] in a neighborhood—that would be ridiculous and redundant and not very cost-effective. . . . We need . . . to fill the gaps in services." Another participant commented, "We need to match needs and assets. . . . We allowed them to use our facility, and they supported us in several ways."

Knowing the community is the fourth key element. One participant, when discussing the importance of not promising "things you can't deliver," commented, "You have to send good emissaries out. . . . You have to send the right kind of people out." This is related to McKnight and Kretzmann's idea (1993) of asset mapping. They believe that communities have assets, such as schools, ethnic and religious organizations, institutions of higher education, hospitals, park departments, and libraries, to name but a few. All of these assets have considerable potential for forming partnerships with schools.

Characteristics of effective partnerships

Respondents in this study agreed that partners have to be *flexible* to be responsive to the needs of children and the systems they serve. By their very nature, effective partnerships change the needs, assets, and resources of those involved. Collaboratives that allow people to change roles, expand functions, and "wear many hats" are those most likely to succeed. As the director of an off-campus program of a community technical college noted when speaking about effective partnerships, "You have to do many things at the same time. . . . You're juggling tasks and responsibilities. You cannot be afraid to do everything that needs to be done in order to get a project completed. . . . You don't get penalized if you fail, because the idea is that you try something you think is a good idea; you go ahead and try it. . . . You have the latitude to do that kind of thing."

Successful partnerships fill the gaps created when organizations provide uncoordinated services. Respondents noted that effective partnerships are experienced as *seamless* by the users of the services they provide. To accomplish this, partners must spend time communicating, mapping assets, and linking resources. Duplication, competition, and contradictory goals and rules are eliminated when partners work in concert.

Respondents found that, in addition to providing a needed service, effective partnerships are *value-added* for their clients and participants. Efficient, synergistic partnerships are creative and constructive for both providers and users of their services. They build internal capacity, and they challenge the partners to grow in new directions. One superintendent described how a mentor program his district pursued with outside agencies and businesses enriched the lives of students, teachers, and the members of the outside organizations.

Institutionalizing partnerships

"If you leave it at the individual level, then it is not going to be successful in the long run. You're not going to institutionalize it." That warning was echoed by several of those interviewed for our study, including the community technical college program director who issued the caveat. The most formidable obstacle to the widespread adoption of educational partnerships is the failure to legitimize school-community collaborations as part of a school's typical service delivery structure. This obstacle limits the use of partnerships as effective and accepted means of providing the full range of services that allow each child to excel in school.

For collaborations to be absorbed into the formal structure of the educational system, it is necessary to gain the commitment of the public and of universities, professional organizations, government agencies, and the business community. A critical first step is to allow individuals who have successfully developed and sustained partnerships within organizations to act as models, mentors, and leaders. Schools must review and revise policies and practices that discourage, limit, or constrain collaboration and build into their standards, training, and certification procedures a culture that teaches and rewards collaboration.

The emerging roles of educational leaders as compradors

In her autobiography, Nien Cheng, a former Chinese political prisoner, discussed the comprador role created in the 1800s to facilitate interactions between the insulated Chinese government and foreign companies. *Comprador*, a Portuguese word used in Maçao, a former Portuguese colony on an island near Hong Kong, literally means "buyer." Compradors were needed because of the bureaucracies and hierarchies pervasive throughout imperial China. Compradors were local Chinese people "who acted as liaisons between foreign firms and Chinese officials" (Cheng, 1986, p. 281). They were fluent in a second language, cognizant of the mores and customs of other cultures, and bi- or multi-lingual and -cultural, enabling them to freely cross boundaries. Without compradors, it would not have been possible for foreign firms to access local Chinese organizations and agencies. The compradors provided the flexibility these businesses needed.

The participants in our interviews discussed the boundary-crossing roles of people involved in educational partnerships. Similar to the compradors of China, educational leaders must be bi- or multi-lingual and -cultural. Although at times this may actually involve speaking another language, it also means being facile with the shared language that is created as different organizations with different cultures come together. Trust is developed, boundaries are crossed, and common agendas are identified; thus reciprocal relationships are formed. Aided by the compradors among us, new ways of communicating will create new collaborative cultures. The task for school leaders is to identify compradors within their organization and give them permission and a reason to travel. Armed with a purpose, with permission to seek out others with whom to form linkages, with the authority to act as leaders, and with the imperative to interact across levels and organizations, these emissaries will offer our schools the hope of conducting business in a not-so-usual way that benefits all students and their families.

Conclusion

Students' needs know no boundaries. Therefore, the services provided for them must cross and merge boundaries if they are to seamlessly fill those needs. Delivering educational services that meet this standard requires a paradigm shift away from an organizational focus (we deliver what we do) to a customer focus (we deliver what you need). It also necessitates a change in organizational culture and structure, the beginnings of which are described here and expanded on in various contexts in subsequent chapters.

Cross-agency and cross-organization collaboratives must be designed and implemented by the compradors among us to fill in the gaps in educational services. Finally, these partnerships must be marketed and their results and benefits publicized so that they may be expanded and so that partnering as a way of meeting the educational needs of students can become institutionalized.

References

Cheng, N. *Life and Death in Shanghai.* New York, N.Y.: Penguin, 1986.
Lerner, R. *America's Youth in Crisis.* Thousand Oaks, Calif.: Sage, 1995.
Lipnack, J., and Stamps, J. *The Teamnet Factor: Bringing the Power of Boundary-Crossing Teams into the Heart of Your Business.* New York: Wiley, 1995.
McKnight, J. L., and Kretzmann, J. P. "Mapping Community Capacity." *Michigan State University Community & Economic Development Program Community News,* winter, (2), 1993, pp. 1–4.
Outtz, J. H. *The Demographics of American Families.* Washington, D.C.: Institute for Educational Leadership, 1993.
Senge, P. *The Fifth Discipline.* New York: Doubleday, 1990.
Stacey, R. *Managing the Unknowable.* San Francisco: Jossey-Bass, 1992.

PAULA A. CORDEIRO *is associate professor at the University of Connecticut and a former principal of the American School of Las Palmas, Spain.*

MARY MONROE - KOLEK, *currently a doctoral student at the University of Connecticut, is the principal of Lebanon High School, Lebanon, Connecticut.*

*Partnerships between schools and families are redefining the
future of the education community. This chapter explores
current practices and future directions for practitioners moving
toward founding a caring community of learners.*

2

Nurturing partnerships between schools and families

Roy M. Seitsinger, Jr.

Change will take people who remember what otherwise
gets lost: That it's not just about building a powerful
America, beating out Japan, or even world-class job
skills; it's about creating a more powerful citizenry and
a more caring one. Even then we'll have lots to argue
about.

Deborah Meier, 1995, p. 184

IN HER BOOK *The Power of Their Ideas,* Deborah Meier (1995) uses
journal entries to relate the essence of her message about her
school. She tells the story of how she successfully hooked up with
a mother whose son had been found selling drugs. Instead of throw-
ing out the same old excuses, the mother agreed with the school's
findings. Meier, celebrating her courage, tells her, "Then, we can
help." The reasons this parent was so receptive could be many, but
Meier attributes her response to years of hard work with the community of parents and students, building trust, demonstrating
commitment, and showing compassion, perseverance, and respect—

NEW DIRECTIONS FOR SCHOOL LEADERSHIP, NO. 2, WINTER 1996 © JOSSEY-BASS PUBLISHERS

all of which brought hope to the situation. Meier's use of *we* does not separate the school from the family, as in "the royal *we*." It is meant to bring the school and family together as one mutually compassionate and understanding entity working to assist the student.

When Principal Daisy Cubais started to walk the neighborhood around Kosciuszk Middle School in Milwaukee, Wisconsin, she sought to make families feel more welcome. However, parents and students viewed her new actions with a jaundiced eye. The reaction Daisy encountered was not surprising. This demonstrates the common view of the relationship between school and home as (at least potentially) adversarial. According to Noddings (1992), "One of the school's most serious shortcomings is that it so consistently induces and maintains the creation of rivals and enemies" (p. 54). How do we develop relationships between schools and families that are supportive and growth-oriented, without producing the rivalry Noddings mentions? Perhaps this question can be answered by recognizing that a fundamental partnership in education exists between the family and the school and that this partnership is unequivocally related to improving children's achievement. If this is the case, schools should be developing comprehensive family involvement plans.

This chapter offers observations regarding the family-school relationship. First, it presents a historical review of family participation and the development of family-school partnerships. It gives examples of formal and informal programs and practices that exemplify successful partnerships, and it describes the motivation behind them and the impact such partnerships may have on school practitioners. This is followed by a discussion of the changing American family, the school as an extended family, the nature of a caring community, and the ways administrators can help educators relate to families and establish a caring community of learners. In an effort to focus administrative thinking and action, the paradigm of a founder is offered as a model for school administrators to use when thinking about how to nurture family involvement.

The importance of family partnerships in education

Research recognizes that students do better, attend school more often, and have fewer attitudinal and behavioral issues when families are involved in the child's education (Henderson and Berla, 1994). In recent years, educational reforms have attempted to build the legitimacy and the quantity of parental involvement (Goldring and Rallis, 1993). Educators are asking parents to participate in curriculum development, staff development, hiring and firing, school governance, and strategic planning (National Parent-Teacher Association, 1992). *The National Education Goals Report* (1994) lists parent participation as its seventh tenet. This report states that schools "will promote partnerships that will increase parental involvement and participation in promoting the social, emotional, and academic growth of children" (p. 11). A review of the development of family involvement in education may show how parents, families, educators, and public policymakers arrived at these conclusions. (Due to changing demographics, the term *family involvement* rather than *parent involvement* is used throughout this chapter.)

A brief history of family involvement in schools

Long ago, when school was held in a one-room building that doubled as the village church and town hall, families deferred to educators on many issues and rarely interfered with curriculum recommendations or school discipline. They did usually have a say in the hiring of the headmaster, however, and the length of the school day and when the school would let the children out to tend the fields. Parents' strongest statement about school priorities and impacts was made when they did not allow their children to attend. In the early 1900s, when school attendance became compulsory and schools began to assume the obligatory aspect they have today, the role of parents changed to the "bake sale" mode (Henderson, 1988). During this period, many educators kept parents at arm's length concerning educational decisions. Parents were asked only to support the school financially through fund-raising activities such as bake sales and book fairs. Professional educators were the decision makers regarding students' education.

In the 1950s and 1960s, a shift from the bake sale mode began to emerge with the organization of the National Association of Retarded Citizens (NARC). NARC marked one of the first times parents organized into a child advocacy group to change daily educational practices. The trend was strengthened with the Supreme Court's desegregation decision in 1954. These public actions were precursors to the establishment of more substantial family involvement in schools. When Head Start was established in 1966, the federal government required that parents constitute a large portion of the controlling body of local programs. Then, in 1975, the Education of Handicapped Children Act shifted the stance of parents further by requiring schools to communicate with parents in certain ways and involve them in all pertinent decisions about their children.

In recent years, parents have been taking more active roles in all aspects of schools. The "parent voice" movement inspired by James Comer of Yale University as well as other researchers has ignited new family- and student-oriented programs focusing on family involvement. Comer (1986) found that more long-term family involvement positively affects educational achievement. He also noted a reduction in absenteeism and in discipline and behavior problems. Comer observed that family involvement programs fostered a sense of trust among teachers, administrators, and parents. Ultimately, family involvement in schools enhances the "shared values" of all human service agencies and families (Redding, 1991). This helps build a feeling of community and positively affects students' ability to learn. If family involvement is most effective when it is comprehensive, long lasting, and well planned, then it would seem to be most powerful when schools work as partners with parents (Melnick and Fiene, 1990).

Henderson (1988) warns that family involvement cannot be considered "a quick fix nor a luxury; it is absolutely fundamental to a healthy system of public education" (p. 153). In spite of the clarion calls for family involvement, after twenty-five years of legislation and support for parent involvement, most states have not taken sufficient action to establish policies and procedures that foster family involvement. Twenty states have passed legislation to increase parent participation; however, most have not passed the kind of legislation that does more than just pay lip service to the idea (Nardine and Morris, 1991).

A key factor that is forcing educators to change their ideas about parent involvement is the increasing realization that the "traditional" American family is a myth. Epstein (1987) argues that it may never have existed. In fact, the American family promulgated by the media and politicians' discussions of family values may only have existed on television. At the height of the male breadwinner, female homemaker family of the 1950s, only 60 percent of American children lived in such families. America has had the highest divorce rate in the world since the turn of the century (Coontz, 1995). Today, many more families have both parents working fulltime. There are major income differences between married couples and single-parent families (Cordeiro, Reagan, and Martinez, 1994). Fewer households have children in school, dropping from 67 percent in 1960 to about 19 percent in 1993 (Tracy, 1995). There is also a substantial difference in the diversity, age, ethnicity, and number of children in the general population (Outtz, 1993). Minority children are more likely to live in single-parent families. Natriello, McDill, and Pallas (1990) state that by the year 2020, students of color will account for about 46 percent of the nation's school population. If these trends continue, the challenge of involving parents and families will become even more difficult.

Programs that focus on school-based family services are a popular mode of response to family involvement, particularly in minority and low-income areas. Vandergrift and Greene (1992) found that parent involvement is most critical (and difficult to attain) with "at-risk" families. Schools need to reach out to low-income and minority families, who often feel intimidated by

school. Many adult family members remember few positive experiences in their own schooling. Often they are not as academically
skilled as higher-income parents, and they may feel inadequate to
the task of advocating for their children in a school environment.
Many families are unfamiliar with the operation, politics, and
bureaucratic practices of schools. Additionally, cultural and language differences are potential barriers. However, strong evidence
suggests that these families are just as committed to their children's
education as are parents from higher-income brackets (Henderson
and Berla, 1994). Lareau (1987) contends that low-income parents
and parents of diverse cultures are just waiting to be approached;
however, part of being approachable is establishing a caring attitude. The establishment of a caring community of learners will
encourage family involvement.

An approach to family involvement

From her many studies of family involvement in education, Epstein
(1994) developed a topology that includes parents as providers of
students' basic needs, communication from school to home, parents working at the school, parents as home instructors, parent
involvement in school governance, and parents as collaborators
with the whole community.

Epstein explains that each of these levels carries different weights
and different consequences for both the parents and the school.
First, the basic obligation of families is to provide a safe and healthy
living environment for their children. Schools can provide information and training to support families in this endeavor. Second,
the basic obligation of schools in this relationship is to establish
two-way communication with the family. Good communication
enhances the family's understanding of the program and curriculum and how students fit into the scheme of schooling. Effective
communications also help the school develop an understanding of
family needs. Third, families can have a substantial impact on the

school. Traditionally, they are active through volunteer activities such as attendance at school events, parent teacher organization meetings, classroom support efforts, one-on-one tutoring, and so on. Epstein's fourth basic obligation of families includes family involvement in learning activities in the home. This involvement can assist in solidifying the youth's understanding of the curriculum and help him or her develop a respect for learning. Fifth, family members who participate in governance decisions enhance their understanding of the daily operations of their children's school and can become contributors to its success. Finally, Epstein's research discusses the importance of families who, through partnering with the school, become collaborators with community organizations that obtain assistance from various support services, such as health care agencies, cultural outreach events, and child care programs. This helps the family provide a more stable environment for children to learn, by linking together people and agencies that can assist children.

Innovative programs

Kagan and Neville (1993) observe that there has been a "proliferation of programs, an expanding interest at the legislative level, and an increasingly widespread public acknowledgment of the need for comprehensive family services" (p. 4). From this proliferation, multifaceted programming has sprung up that inspires and even defines local communities and their commitment to children, schools, and families.

When the programming format is considered, family partnerships may be broken down into three broad areas: community-based efforts, general models of family involvement, and individual efforts. The most visible and largest area is the publicly recognizable, well-organized, and well-publicized partnerships between the school and the community. Programs such as New Beginnings in San Diego, the Denver Family Resource Schools in Denver,

Colorado, and the Child Opportunity Zones of Rhode Island are examples of large, visible programs that affect schools and families. These programs often receive national or strong local media attention. Brief descriptions of each of these programs are provided here as outstanding examples of school-family partnerships and service integration.

New Beginnings

Started in 1988, San Diego's New Beginnings program was developed through the collaboration of nine agencies and businesses to improve the web of services offered to families. This group's focus was not only educational but centered on the needs of the family as a whole. It targeted elementary school children and their families. The agencies were expected to leave behind their restrictive bureaucratic attitudes and practices and attempt to meet the full range of family needs. After three years of work in three portable classrooms on the grounds of the Hamilton Elementary School, the New Beginnings Center for Children and Families program has expanded to other schools and school systems.

Denver Family Resource Schools

This project relied on the work of Dr. Edward Ziegler of Yale University and on a program already under way in Denver. In 1989 the Family Resource Schools (FRS), in Denver, Colorado, were designated in a request for proposals issued by a project planning team made up of representatives from the Denver public schools, the mayor's office, and various foundations. These schools' focus is on providing traditional academic programming and family-centered programs. The goal of the program is to remove barriers and to allow students and families to interact with schools by expanding hours and access. The FRS schools emphasize five areas: student achievement, adult education, parent education, family support services, and staff development and training. Principals serve a key role by mediating conflicts; being accountable for student, teacher, and parent relationships; and supporting a balanced effort toward improving learning.

Child Opportunity Zones

In March 1992, the state of Rhode Island published *Educating All Our Children: The Report of the 21st Century Education Commission.* This report advocated parent involvement and the linking of education and social service agencies to the needs of parents and the expanding mission of schools. State-level planners identified financial support through several agencies, including the Rhode Island Department of Education, the United Way, and the Rhode Island Department of Health. Facilitators were available to initiate programs and activities that would bring families into schools and support them in numerous ways, such as offering referral services to outside agencies, simplifying application processes so that families would not have to duplicate efforts between support agencies, and extending school hours. Nineteen original sights were chosen; all provided a different sort of support, depending on the needs of the local community.

Individual impact

Individual efforts like the work of Deborah Meier and Daisy Cubais are establishing another kind of family partnership. Whether these partnerships germinated from some larger effort or are the result of a small group coming together, they all have one individual who provides cohesion and sparks continued effort. These partnerships may or may not receive attention outside their communities. Nevertheless, they can represent sincere efforts by principals, teachers, parents, or others to change the way schools interact and to support families at the local level. The individual efforts of an educator working with a parent or a student and his or her family to improve the child's school experience should not be discounted.

School administrators should be aware of three types of programming frameworks: community-based efforts, general models of family involvement, and individual initiatives. Understanding these types of programming approaches helps administrators integrate a vast array of educational innovations, community demands, and student expectations.

Caring communities

Traditionally, improvements to curriculum, instruction, and classroom management were built around the idea that the individual teacher, the individual student, and their relationship with each other is irrelevant to the success of instruction (Noddings, 1992). The relationship between schools and families were viewed the same way. This runs contrary to what practitioners and families are expressing in the programs and practices discussed here. The overriding factor found in the research supporting parent and family involvement is caring. Caring for the well-being of children and their families should be the number one priority for all family partnership strategists. Caring emphasizes partnership, mutual respect, and the growth of competent, caring, loving, and lovable people (Noddings, 1995).

Starratt (1991) proposes three ethical themes that schools should cultivate to support the development of caring communities: justice, critiquing, and caring. School administrators are responsible for enhancing the themes of justice, critiquing, and caring in their community. Educators and family members can achieve caring communities if they sustain a clear understanding and continuity of purpose when interacting with each other and society (Noddings, 1991). What is most pertinent in the concept of caring is a set of beliefs on the part of the administrator that he or she must engender to the community.

The role of building administrators

Chavkin and Williams (1987) believe that the job of establishing a caring school environment and interacting with the community has become too large for an individual administrator to manage. Bempechat (1990) found that when teachers and school administrators are "strongly committed to drawing parents into their children's education, the academic outcomes for children can be very positive" (p. 11). Schools need not function in isolation. Thus, the notion of partnerships simply makes sense for all involved.

A building administrator who wishes to carry out a local family involvement strategy or a large family-school partnership program should carefully consider the environment in which he or she will set up this innovation. Developing a clear mental picture of how to integrate a family-school partnership program into the school's current programming is crucial. There is a need for administrators to look beyond traditional ways of working with parents and families. Collaborating with parents to develop a clear statement about the goals of family involvement in school is one step building administrators might take. They could ask parents how they want to be involved with their children's education. Based on the interests of parents, a variety of opportunities could be made available for family involvement. If educators listen carefully to the community, they will ensure that parents are more fully involved at all levels of the educational system.

How can a building administrator accomplish this? Researchers have offered many analogies to clarify building administrators' roles. Building administrators are described as instructional leaders, managers, counselors, head learners, coaches, facilitators, mentors, boundary spanners, and change agents. All these roles can be overwhelming. A building administrator once told me that, "You read the literature of what a good principal is, and it can be just a little daunting." Another colleague asked, "How can I be all these things?" However, this is linear thinking; somehow administrators need to move from being boundary spanners to facilitators and then instructional leaders, drawing on different pieces of knowledge for each area. Building administrators cannot accomplish this kind of multitasking if they think of the models as separate and distinct ideas associated with separate and distinct actions. Chavkin and Williams (1987) advise that step 1 in trying to comprehend this task is to build a basis for understanding. Developing a clear model that conceptually organizes the tasks required of building administrators for the next century can establish a basis for understanding.

Investigators have offered additional analogies to describe the role of principals in recent years. Sergiovanni (1992) presents the concept of the servant leader and steward, in which the principal develops a trusting relationship with the school constituencies, and they in turn entrust him or her to fulfill certain obligations. Goldring and Rallis (1993) define boundary spanners in education as building administrators who contact people outside their own group. Their job is to convey influence between groups and to represent perceptions, expectations, and ideas to all parties. This concept assumes that traditional boundaries separating schools from communities have been weakened or removed. Goldring and Rallis (1993) propose that the principals of dynamic schools are "in-charge" principals, and they attempt to pull in many of the roles described above as they advocate for placing the building administrator in charge. However, the question may be, does the building administrator need to be in charge? Perhaps the founder analogy better depicts and clarifies some of these tasks.

Building administrators as founders

Family partnerships are a major part of the school reform movement. The key to family partnerships is the leadership of the building administrator and the commitment of the community. A paradigm of building administrator as founder encapsulates several of the oft-described roles building administrators assume and crystallizes the notions and actions needed to deal with family involvement programming.

Martin, Sitkin, and Boehm (1983) have discussed founders in the corporate world. To these authors, a founder is an individual who begins an enterprise or develops a corporate entity. The concept of founder offered in this chapter is more complex. Picture a group of settlers setting out for the New World. They are led by an individual (or even a small group) who has only a vague picture of where they are going but a clear picture of where they do *not* want to be. They are willing to take risks and to consider imaginative alternatives, because of their desire to somehow improve their lot. The founder is the person who is seen throughout the passage to the New World as the moral and spiritual leader, a leader who sustains the group's purpose but does not oppress them.

A founder knows his or her place in the environment—in the big picture—and is able to locate the most desirable position of the group or organization within the environment as well. A founder is able to sustain effort, to look ahead, to delegate, and, often, to move aside and allow others to decide and to take risks. He or she encourages others and is able to offer a sense of purpose and safety. This person maintains the vision; he or she is an individual who can facilitate, manage, and coach. A founder is a flag bearer and flag planter. When the shores of the New World are within sight, the founder calls out, "Land ho!" and steps aside, allowing others to expand their roles. When the community is newly established, the founder contributes to establishing and maintaining a citizenry of caring individuals who will maintain their commitment. The legend of the founder can also sustain the community over time.

The building administrator, like a corporate founder, sustains the purpose of the enterprise (in this case, an educational partnership) and exhibits all of the above behaviors. The building-administrator-as-founder is the welcomer. He or she is the person who ensures that families, teachers, and students appreciate one another and communicate with one another in a valuable way focused on children and learning.

Conclusion

Parent involvement and family partnerships can be a powerful reform tool for use by building administrators, and building administrators are not alone. The clarion call for family involvement comes from all corners of our community and will not go unheeded. The partnership of school and family is fundamental to the growth and achievement of children. Schools have a wealth of community members to draw on as we attempt to found caring school communities that will produce the citizenry of the next century.

References

Bempechat, J. *The Role of Parent Involvement in Children's Academic Achievement: A Review of the Literature.* ERIC, Trends and Issues no. 14. Washington, D.C.: U.S. Department of Education, Institute for Urban and Minority Education, ERIC Clearinghouse on Urban Education, 1990.

Chavkin, N. F., and Williams, D. L., Jr. *Families and Schools in a Pluralistic Society.* Albany: State University of New York Press, 1987.

Comer, J. P. "Parent Participation in the Schools." *Phi Delta Kappan,* 1986, 67, 442–446.

Coontz, S. "The Way We Weren't: The Myth and Reality of the 'Traditional' Family." *National Forum,* 1995, 75, 11–14.

Cordeiro, P., Reagan, T., and Martinez, L. P. *Multiculturalism and TQE: Addressing Cultural Diversity in Schools.* Thousand Oaks, Calif.: Corwin Press, 1994.

Epstein, J. *School and Family Partnerships: Preparing Educators and Improving Schools.* Boulder, Colo.: Westview, 1994.

Epstein, J. L. "Parent Involvement: What Research Says to Administrators." *Education and Urban Society,* 1987, 19, 119–136.

Goldring, E. B., and Rallis, S. F. *Principals of Dynamic Schools: Taking Charge of Change.* Thousand Oaks, Calif.: Corwin Press, 1993.

Henderson, A. *The Evidence Continues to Grow: Parent Involvement Improves Student Achievement.* Columbia, Md.: National Committee for Citizens in Education, 1988.

Henderson, A., and Berla, N. (eds.). *A New Generation of Evidence: The Family Is Critical to Student Achievement.* Columbia, Md.: Center for Law and Education, 1994.

Kagan, S. L., and Neville, P. R. "Family Support and School-Linked Services: Variations on a Theme." In K. Goetz (ed.), *Family Resource Coalition Report: Family Support and School-Linked Services.* Chicago: Family Resource Coalition, 1993.

Lareau, A. "Social Class Differences in Family-School Relationships: The Importance of Cultural Capital." *Sociology of Education,* 1987, 60, 73–85.

Martin, J., Sitkin, S., and Boehm, M. *Wild-Eyed Guys and Old Salts: The Emergence and Disappearance of Organizational Subcultures.* Working paper, Stanford University Graduate School of Business, 1983.

Meier, D. *The Power of Their Ideas: Lessons for America from a Small School in Harlem.* Boston: Beacon Press, 1995.

Melnick, S., and Fiene, R. "Assessing Parents' Attitudes Toward School Effectiveness." Paper presented at the annual meeting of the American Educational Research Association, Boston, April 16–20, 1990.

Nardine, F. E., and Morris, R. D. "Parent Involvement in the States: How Firm Is the Commitment?" *Phi Delta Kappan*, 1991, *72*, 363–366.

National Education Goals Panel. *The National Education Goals Report: Building a Nation of Learners*. Washington, D.C.: U.S. Government Printing Office, 1994.

National Parent-Teacher Association. *For Our Children: Parents and Families in Education—Results of the National Parent Involvement Summit*. Washington, D.C.: National Parent-Teacher Association, 1992.

Natriello, G., McDill, E., and Pallas, A. M. *Schooling the Disadvantaged*. New York: Teachers College Press, 1990.

Noddings, N. "Caring and Continuity in Education." *Scandinavian Journal of Educational Research*, 1991, *35*, 3–12.

Noddings, N. *The Challenge to Care in Schools: An Alternative Approach to Education*. New York: Teachers College Press, 1992.

Noddings, N. "A Morally Defensible Mission for Schools in the 21st Century." *Phi Delta Kappan*, 1995, *76*, 65–68.

Outtz, J. H. *The Demographics of American Families*. Washington, D.C.: Institute for Educational Leadership, 1993.

Redding, S. "Creating a School Community Through Parent Involvement." *The Education Digest*, 1991, *57*, 6–9.

Sergiovanni, T. J. *Moral Leadership: Getting to the Heart of School Improvement*. Jossey-Bass: San Francisco, 1992.

Starratt, R. J. "Building an Ethical School: A Theory for Practice in Educational Leadership." *Educational Administration Quarterly*, 1991, *27*, 185–202.

Tracy, J. R. "Family: Involving Families in Student Achievement." *Schools in the Middle*. National Association of Secondary School Principals, November-December 1995.

Vandergrift, J. A., and Greene, A. L. "Rethinking Parent Involvement." *Educational Leadership*, 1992, *50*(1), 57–60.

ROY M. SEITSINGER, JR., *is an elementary school principal on sabbatical leave at the University of Connecticut in Storrs, Connecticut, where he is a doctoral student in the Department of Educational Leadership.*

This chapter discusses the trends in partnerships between schools and institutions of higher education. It describes several existing partnerships as well as the potential barriers to developing such collaborations.

3

Partnerships between schools and institutions of higher education

L. Nan Restine

INSTITUTIONS OF HIGHER EDUCATION ARE NATURAL PARTNERS for schools. Despite teachers' and administrators' wariness of academic elitism and uneasiness about the use of research and theory, there is more agreement between schools and universities about educational matters than either fully realizes (Jones and Maloy, 1988). Building instructional capacity is the fundamental rationale for developing partnerships with institutions of higher education. Capacity may be enhanced by improving the performance of individuals, by adding resources, by restructuring work, and by restructuring how services are delivered.

This chapter addresses the following questions: What are the traditions and trends in collaborations between schools and institutions of higher education? What are some of the problems and possibilities?

NEW DIRECTIONS FOR SCHOOL LEADERSHIP, NO. 2, WINTER 1996 © JOSSEY-BASS PUBLISHERS

Traditions and trends

Partnerships between schools and institutions of higher education are not a new idea. They can be traced to the birth of public education and the vested interest of teacher training institutions in common schools. Tracing the history of these partnerships reveals many instances of collaboration where powerful teaching and learning were paramount and adaptivity and continuous renewal were hallmarks.

Two major trends have developed in recent years. As these trends have expanded, they have developed more and more similar characteristics. One involves forming professional communities between schools and universities, resulting in contextualized theory and theoretically informed practice (Darling-Hammond and McLaughlin, 1995). This has been the focus of professional development schools in particular. Second, there is a strong belief that efforts at professional collaboration and service integration are incomplete without professional pre-service and in-service education. Certain examples across the country reflect a blending of these trends.

The National Center for Social Work and Education Collaboration, founded by Fordham University with support from the DeWitt Wallace–*Reader's Digest* fund, assists projects carried out by a national network of universities (graduate schools of social work and education) and public school sites. In this partnership, graduate students work together to provide needed services to children and families in public schools. The center also sponsors an annual conference, publishes yearly reports and newsletters, and supports a Web site.

Wayne State University's College of Education and School of Social Work have entered into a collaborative project in Michigan's first charter school. The focus of this collaboration is on the joint training of social work and education interns and on furthering the efforts of teachers and social workers to meet the academic, social, psychological, and health needs of their community's children and families. The ultimate goal of the project is to help families and communities make a difference in students' academic achievement.

Throughout the nation there are now a growing number of "professional development schools." Originally conceived by the Holmes Group, a consortium of universities with teacher training programs, these partnerships have also resulted in books, such as *Tomorrow's Teachers* (Holmes Group, 1986), *Tomorrow's Schools* (Holmes Group, 1990), and *Tomorrow's Schools of Education* (Holmes Group, 1995). One example is the Professional Development Center formed by the Hartford, Connecticut, public schools and the University of Connecticut. This collaboration among school professionals and university faculty and students is designed to enhance public education through supervised clinical experiences for teachers and other education professionals. Teachers, school and university administrators, faculty, university students, and community agencies work together to foster the growth of all parties. Specifically, the center attempts to provide an optimal environment for student learning and personal self-fulfillment, to provide opportunities for pre-service preparation and career-long professional development, and to conduct collaborative research and development activities that advance theory and practice in urban education.

Partnerships can also be found between schools and higher education institutions that do not have schools or colleges of education. For example, the Yale–New Haven Teachers Institute, established in 1978, is a partnership of Yale University and the New Haven public schools. This partnership is designed to strengthen teaching and improve student learning in the humanities and the sciences. The institute is an interschool, interdisciplinary forum for Yale faculty and school teachers that integrates curriculum development and intellectual renewal. Yale also supports a collaborative program at New Haven's Career High School, Yale–New Haven Hospital, and Yale School of Medicine and Nursing. This program emphasizes early exposure for students to career opportunities in the fields of allied health, business, and computer technology. The partnership encourages interaction between faculty and staff at the School of Medicine and Nursing and Yale–New Haven Hospital and students and teachers at Career High School, and it reflects their mutual commitment to health care, academic excellence, and community service.

An example of an interprofessional partnership is the University of Washington's Training for Interprofessional Collaboration project. This is a graduate program involving the schools of Social Work, Nursing, Education, Public Affairs, and Public Health and Community Medicine. The underlying theme of this partnership is that universities seeking to prepare professionals for interprofessional collaboration must themselves be collaborative and interprofessional. Thus it demands of the university and its faculty the same kinds of skills, attitudes, and knowledge that are expected of human service professionals in the field.

These are but a few examples of the kind of partnerships that are reinventing and revitalizing education across the country. Typically, initiatives such as these begin with the recognition on the part of school and related health and helping professionals of the vulnerability of poor children, youth, and families in their community. New visions and missions for interprofessional collaboration and service integration in community schools and agencies are then matched by those schools' and agencies' counterparts in higher education, interprofessional education programs.

Whether by choice or by mandate, schools and universities are faced with new questions about their mission and vision. School and university leaders confront competing missions and goals driven by internal and external constituencies. However, these dilemmas provide opportunities. As Lawson and Hooper-Briar (1994, p. 18) suggest, "Placed at center stage ... the needs of children, youth and families allow a planning strategy aimed at unification, coherence, and constituency building."

Partnership initiatives can have domino effects in higher education, schools, and communities. Consider the following examples (Lawson and Hooper-Briar, 1994):

- *Land grant institutions.* The ideal behind the creation of the land grant colleges was to create universities for the people, institutions that would be responsive to societal needs and aspirations.

Therefore, these institutions are particularly well suited to address public school education, economic development, and reform of undergraduate and graduate education. The problems and needs of children, youth, and families are not unique to urban areas. Through interprofessional collaboration and service integration, partnerships involving agricultural services can dovetail with public school science classes, student apprenticeships at museums or plant nurseries, and other programs.

- *Community colleges.* Community colleges are expected to attend to local needs, and they are especially responsible for providing their community members with practical knowledge and skills. Programs in community colleges can serve as "lighthouse" projects for child care, early childhood education, and parent and community programs. These programs can be consumer-guided and delivered where their beneficiaries play vital roles in the community's schools, agencies, and neighborhoods.

- *Urban colleges and universities.* At the University of Pennsylvania, for example, the public school is viewed as the best place to do the work aimed at community revitalization and the needs of children, youth, and families. Initiatives do not have to replace traditional activities, but they can enlarge them through academically based community service programs that are responsive to community needs and have the potential to influence curriculum and policy.

- *Professional schools, colleges, and departments.* The needs of children, youth, and families justify the involvement of the helping professions of health care and social work in educational collaborations. Likewise, the economic development of communities may be accelerated by the involvement of business schools. The potential and professional boundaries are limitless if the notion of specialization, particularly among academic disciplines, is reconsidered in terms of commonalties and interdependence. Few disciplines alone provide all of the knowledge and understanding necessary to substantially improve outcomes through school-university partnerships. More cross-disciplinary and cross-professional partnerships in higher education are needed.

School and university leaders who make such initiatives an institutional priority can set the stage for pervasive change. Costs are escalating for those colleges and universities that are intent upon isolating themselves from their surroundings. Furthermore, through enlightened leadership, those once thought of as clients can become full-fledged colleagues and partners.

Problems and possibilities

Getting beyond doing things better, smarter, or differently is not easy. Although institutional and individual renewal are worthy endeavors, achieving renewal by operating in isolation is unreasonable. The problems and possibilities of developing genuine partnerships between schools and institutions of higher education can be explored through the need for a shared purpose and vision. However, norms in schools and universities differ. Universities value norms based on generalizations about schools and teaching, and schools prefer norms that have an application in a material context. Schools and universities have mutual self-interests; they are not independent entities. However, serious dialogue between them about their enterprises is, all too often, an uncommon event.

The classic and perennial problems of responsibility, authority, and ideologies of control are manifested in attempts to establish inter- or intra-organizational relationships. Institutional cultures shape understandings, perspectives, and expectations and enable routine and predictable behaviors to become institutionalized. The prevailing culture of schools and universities has limited our vision about the kinds of partnerships and communities that can reduce organizational and institutional barriers. Knapp and others (1993) note that collaborative interprofessional practice challenges the fundamental assumptions underlying professional education in the university. Faculty reflect disciplinary loyalty and allegiance, and even with a strong guiding vision, conflicts arise involving status, rewards, and career goals. The reward structure of universities, and to some degree that of schools, thwarts collaborative efforts. There is a need to develop new criteria for tenure and promotion of professors who work in partnerships with schools. Additionally, the organizational structure and underlying values of institutions of higher education have limited professors' ability to work as a team and do interdisciplinary work. Goodlad, Soder, and Sirotnik (1990) mention that the closer professors get to working with practitioners, the less prestige and security they have within their institution. However, this conventional wisdom is undergoing revision in some institutions, since building better connections and collaborative inquiry offer great promise for producing and implementing knowledge in context.

Klein (1990) proposes seven predictable barriers to consider when developing interprofessional collaborations:

1. *The illusion of consensus.* The participants reach agreement prematurely, ignoring issues of complexity, core values, and vision.
2. *Failure to negotiate a common working vocabulary.* The participants maintain their disciplinary roles; people withdraw to the familiar.
3. *Open conflict over status.* The participants fight over their place in the collaborative. Such conflicts may be self-perpetuating.
4. *Too large a group.* Involving more than four or five disciplines inhibits creativity and aggravates communication problems, encouraging work at the lowest common denominator.
5. *Equating mission with vision.* Seeing collaboration, service integration, and interprofessional education as ends in themselves.
6. *Neglecting the need for designated leadership.* Assuming that everyone is, and wants to be, the leader.
7. *Failing to involve students, faculty, parents, and practitioners.* This is the price of arrogance.

Before appropriate structures and reward systems can be designed, other issues must be addressed, such as what interprofessional collaboration will accomplish; under what conditions, how, when, and why the participants will collaborate; who may participate; what kinds of work activities will be undertaken; and how roles will change. Consider what Lawson and Hooper-Briar (1994) suggest as shared elements of a guiding vision for higher education institutions and their school and community partners:

- *A theory of social development* that is context-sensitive and includes the roles of schools, families, and health and human services agencies in improving the quality of life and learning.
- *A theory of organizational renewal and change*, including a theory of *power* (that addresses who has it and how, when, where, and why it is distributed and used), a theory of *partnerships* (that explains the ways partnerships are formed, maintained, and expanded), and a theory of *institutionalization* (describing how the partnership will proceed beyond the status of a project or pilot).
- *A theory of language and communication* that informs the way people will frame and name their work.
- *A theory of education and constituency building* that includes strategies for gaining, enfranchising, and empowering participants.
- *A theory of leadership* to guide the participants in deciding who will assume responsibility; under what conditions, when, and why they will assume it; and what constitutes transformative, collaborative leadership.
- *A theory of assessment, evaluation, and research* that details the relationships and necessary distinctions involved.
- *The core or bedrock values* that define the essence of the work and provide consistency, cohesiveness, and a source of renewal.

Establishing school-university partnerships begins with efforts to foster awareness. Subsequently, the challenge becomes one of fostering individual and collective commitment. Sustaining school-university relationships requires leadership that strikes a balance between centralized and decentralized authority and control. Most importantly, however, leadership of school-university partnerships must be shared; it is a more complex undertaking, requiring a balanced perspective, mutual responsibility, and authentic relationships. Establishing partnerships extends the environment and provides access to resources in less tentative ways. At the very least, leadership for partnership development means embracing uncertainty, complexity, and ambiguity in the incipient stages if meaningful improvement and renewal of schools and universities is to occur.

Conclusion

Developing genuine partnerships between schools and institutions of higher education depends on realizing that many, if not most, of the problems and issues confronting schools, universities, and communities have a common connection. Operating in isolation and making decisions unilaterally does little to overcome traditional "pecking orders" and "plantation mentalities." Partnerships must be focused on particulars and action (Maeroff, 1983). If the main goal of forming educational partnerships is to provide better and additional opportunities for children and adults to learn, then it behooves all educators to explore long-term relationships between and among all levels of educational institutions.

References

Darling-Hammond, L., and McLaughlin, M. "Policies That Support Professional Development in an Era of Reform." *Educational Leadership*, 1995, 76(8), 597–604.

Goodlad, J., Soder, R., and Sirotnik, K. A. (eds.). *Places Where Teachers Are Taught.* San Francisco: Jossey-Bass, 1990.

Holmes Group. *Tomorrow's Teachers.* East Lansing, Mich.: Holmes Group, 1986.

Holmes Group. *Tomorrow's Schools.* East Lansing, Mich.: Holmes Group, 1990.

Holmes Group. *Tomorrow's Schools of Education.* East Lansing, Mich.: Holmes Group, 1995.

Jones, B., and Maloy, R. *Partnerships for Improving Schools.* Westport, Conn.: Greenwood Press, 1988.

Klein, J. *Interdisciplinarity: History, Theory, and Practice.* Detroit: Wayne State University Press, 1990.

Knapp, M., and others. "University-Based Preparation for Collaborative Inter-professional Practice." *Politics of Education Yearbook*, 1993, pp. 137–151.

Lawson, H., and Hooper-Briar, K. "Expanding Partnerships: Involving Colleges and Universities in Interprofessional Collaboration and Service Integration." Oxford, Ohio: Danforth Foundation and Institute for Educational Renewal, 1994.

Maeroff, G. *School and College: Partnering in Education.* Princeton, N.J.: Carnegie Foundation for the Advancement of Teaching, 1983.

L. NAN RESTINE *is assistant professor in the Department of Educational Administration and Higher Education at Oklahoma State University, Stillwater.*

This chapter explores working relationships between health and human services professionals and educators and identifies factors that promote collaborative attitudes and behaviors. The author describes strategies used by principals as key factors in facilitating partnerships and levels of understanding between school-based health center staff and teachers.

4

Strategies for fostering partnerships between educators and health and human services professionals

Ellen Smith Sloan

POOR HEALTH IN AMERICA'S UNDERSERVED YOUTH, inaccessibility to health care and often health insurance, and serious concerns about the welfare of children have been "external shocks" (Jehl and Kirst, 1992, p. 97) to this country for over two centuries. Remediation for these shocks has often involved the public school system: "In 1839 Horace Mann voiced the need for schools to give attention to health" (Cortese, 1993, p. 21). As early as 1840 the populace of Concord, Massachusetts, "requested that physicians provide health care in their schools, just as they provided health care in other public institutions" (Kirby and Lovick, 1987, p. 139).

Although concern was voiced during this time, it was not until the Progressive period (1890 to 1920) and its massive waves of immigration that groups and individuals from many walks of life became cognizant of the plight of children and actually began to

NEW DIRECTIONS FOR SCHOOL LEADERSHIP, NO. 2, WINTER 1996 © JOSSEY-BASS PUBLISHERS

suggest that the public schools play a more significant role in helping them: "Activist writers like Jacob Riis . . . cast a bright light on the suffering of children—the wasting of a generation—and cried out for action" (Tyack, 1992, p. 20). Children's health issues have again found their way to the schoolhouse door—and to an even greater extent than in the past—in the form of school-based health centers (SBHCs). With the birth of this phenomenon in Cambridge, Massachusetts, in 1967, where five distinct health and human services agencies were actually placed within the public elementary school facilities, the concept has grown and developed to significant proportions. As of 1994, over 574 SBHCs can be found in over thirty-three states (Portner, 1994), with new sites being established regularly. Indeed, the idea of using public schools as the "best" sites for administering health and human services to children and youth has become increasingly popular in this country (Zigler, Kagan, and Klugman, 1983).

As this concept takes hold in more and more communities, one finds an increase in the number of handbooks, guides, and reports that discuss establishing SBHCs, including guidelines for funding and policy, suggestions for site selection, and so on. However, research and conversations pertaining to the more intrinsic "human process issues" (Cummings and Worley, 1993, p. 164) implied in these collaboratives and partnerships are sparse and much more recent. In a study of twenty-five collaborative service sites, Hooper-Briar and Lawson (1994) illustrate the importance of this type of research. They speak of the "well-intentioned language of collaboration" (p. 28) and the challenges that diverse professions face when they attempt to "mesh their programs, support, and services into seamless systems" (p. 9). Dryfoos (1994) attempts to inject some humor into these complexities, commenting that collaboration is inherently "an unnatural act between nonconsenting adults" (p. 149).

Social indicators point to the fact that collaborative services for children and youth will continue to grow, and national surveys indicate that community health centers are more frequently located within public schools than in other facilities (Waszak and Neidell,

1991). Observing these trends, I designed a study to explore and clarify these important human process issues. Using case study methodology, I studied four elementary school health centers in four separate urban communities in the Northeast. The project provided a vehicle for observing, explaining, understanding, and describing the complexities of a growing phenomenon. It examined the relationships and interactions among professionals working within public schools, described whether or not collaborative behaviors and attitudes were present, and cataloged the salient factors that accounted for the presence or absence of collaborative behavior.

In attempts to accurately capture the essence of the working relationships at each of the four sites, I conducted in-depth interviews and focus groups with adults from all professions within the actual school settings. These included teachers, nurse practitioners, social workers, principals, superintendents, school nurses, outreach workers, physicians' assistants, and clerical staff. I then triangulated interview and focus group data with data from my observations and data from SBHC documents. An ongoing analysis of data gathered from the four sites has yielded intriguing results pertaining to expected human behaviors, as well as to the subtle and less tangible aspects of human nature.

As health and human services professionals talked about their newly configured work environments and educators discussed incorporating SBHCs into academic settings, four salient themes emerged (see Sloan, 1995). Two of these themes, *a societal imperative* and *boundary-spanning individuals*, are explained in this chapter. Additionally, two models of educational collaboration are presented. The first delineates specific leadership strategies utilized over the course of various phases of SBHC development. These strategies were found to enhance and strengthen the working relationships among adults from diverse professions (see Figure 4.1). The second model depicts a holistic view of the two themes as they relate to the role of the school principal, weaving together components aimed at creating an empathic professional culture within the school building (see Figure 4.2).

Phase I INTRODUCTION	*Phase II* IMPLEMENTATION	*Phase III* INTEGRATION
Screening of teacher applicants for collaborative dispositions	Welcome breakfasts	Monitoring the school environment for questions, confusion, frustration, lack of understanding, and reminders about why the SBHC is in the school
One-on-one meetings with principal, teacher, and new SBHC staff member →	Logo contests	
	Dedication ceremonies	
	Classroom introductions of new SBHC staff person →	Individual classroom presentations of SBHC staff person's specific role in the school
Exploration of confidentiality and referral issues →	Implementation of processes for each →	Monitoring and refinement of process
Team building for teachers and new SBHC staff →	Monitoring and follow-up of team building →	
Faculty meetings prior to creation of SBHC →	Faculty meetings to introduce SBHC staff →	Faculty meetings to explain SBHC programs, discuss issues, ask questions
School newsletter with story about forthcoming SBHC →	Newsletter spotlighting new professionals in the school (educators and health and human services) →	Ongoing newsletter articles
Formalization of principal's knowledge about roles and responsibilities of health and human services professionals →	Facilitation of teachers' knowledge about children's physical and mental health issues, as well as SBHC staff's knowledge of academic issues →	Ongoing awareness of the need to create opportunities for informal and formal interaction among all professionals in the building
Proactive relationship with media		
Proactive participation in funding and space issues —	Ongoing monitoring of funding, staffing, and space concerns —	Intervention techniques and "laying down the law"

Figure 4.1. **Boundary-Spanning Leadership Strategies and the Phases of Collaborative Service Development.**

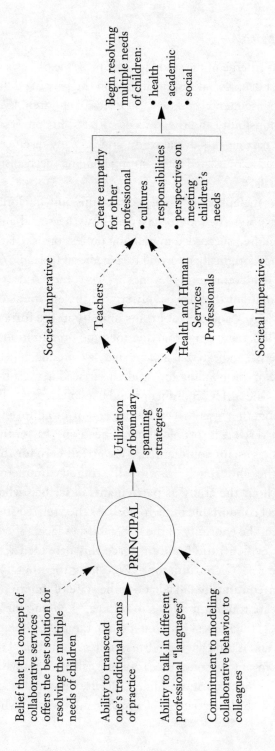

Figure 4.2. Creating an Empathic Professional Culture to Resolve the Complex Needs of Children.

45

A societal imperative

The first theme to emerge in the study was the presence of "a societal imperative," a deep social responsibility on the part of adults to satisfy the immense mental and physical needs of children. Evidence of this responsibility and these needs surfaced in conversations with all the participants in the study, and in many instances the societal imperative translated into a strong bonding mechanism among professionals.

Applying Clark's metaphor (1965) of a saga to this unifying force became the most poignant way to describe how the social and health needs of children succeeded in unifying professionals. Clark writes that the "saga, originally referring to a medieval Icelandic or Norse account of achievements and events . . . has come to mean a . . . unique development that has deeply stirred the emotions of participants" (p. 373), "a powerful means of unity in the formal place . . . making links across internal divisions and organizational boundaries as internal and external groups share a common belief" (p. 381). Evidence of this bonding for children surfaced in most in-depth interviews. One SBHC coordinator said her colleagues' willingness to pull together was driven by the extent of children's multiple needs: "Everyone is sort of willing to bend one way or the other." A medical assistant commented, "We are all here for the same reasons—the children." Emotionally tinged comments appeared throughout the study as participants described what caused them to feel comfortable in their work. As they related stories about children, the enormity of the societal issues facing them was consistently evident; the bonding force this provided was described by one SBHC coordinator as "meshing together." A nurse practitioner continually talked about the state of inner-city children: "There are tons of problems to resolve." Echoing these sentiments was a school nurse: "It's overwhelming in this building. I can see one kid, and it can take forty-five minutes by the time I'm done. And that takes into account the six phone calls I might have to make to find one member of the family." Reality impacted at an even deeper level with the statement of a physician's assistant who candidly described that she can only *attempt* to ameliorate children's health needs brought about by social conditions: "The needs are huge—overwhelming—and we cannot meet them in any way. We can only attempt! The problems at this school are just unbelievable because of combinations of poverty, the family, and living in the city. The energy these kids have to put into their lives is very discouraging. The social problems here are just terrible."

An SBHC coordinator discussed a particularly stressful day with needy children, a day during which she observed the SBHC staff in action: "I've seen people rally around each other—instead of 'I work here, you work there,' and so on. Although they all work independently in a sense, they all mesh to serve the whole child." Many of these conversations reaffirm the research of Trist (1977) and his discussions of "the turbulent environment" (p. 271) and how diverse organizations working in unpredictable and complex settings develop "a higher level of interdependence" (p. 272).

Interdependence and bonding between SBHC staff and teachers were found to vary slightly from site to site and appeared to be dependent on one or both of the following factors: a principal who exhibited boundary-spanning strategies, and one-to-one interaction of teachers with SBHC staff. Teachers in three of the four case study sites with a boundary-spanning principal reported higher comfort levels and understandings regarding the goals and activities of the SBHC, thus creating a feeling of unity with other professionals (discussed further below). At the fourth site, only teachers with students who utilized the SBHC expressed these high comfort levels. As this discussion pertained to the theme of a societal imperative, however, all teachers interviewed verbalized their support for the SBHC and acknowledged its necessity in resolving students' mental and physical health problems. One scenario was described by a SBHC coordinator, following the introduction of a new health center social worker to the school faculty. He commented on his observations of teachers: "The faces of every one of those teachers just kind of lit up with something between joy and desperation, and said, basically, in their varying terms, 'Thank God you're here.'" A teacher from this same faculty explained, "We have an extremely needy group of children here. For most of them, the health clinic is the only health care they get." A teacher with students who regularly utilized the SBHC remarked, "The problems, the crises that come up. I can't do it. There are so many more components to education now as opposed to the way it used to be. As a teacher you wear so many more hats than when I became a teacher fifteen years ago. It's totally different. I can't do it alone."

Taking this theme to yet another level, analysis of data also yielded an even higher stage of sophistication in regard to the bonding and unity among individuals at the SBHCs. It was clear from observations and conversations that in addition to the day-to-day collaboration on services, there was evidence of spontaneous and rapid collaboration among all professionals, regardless of high or low comfort levels. This spontaneity and rapidity occurred during times of crisis and was reported by participants in all four sites. These crisis situations, almost instantaneous manifestations of the societal imperative, appeared to dictate behavior. A district coordinator of an SBHC noted, "If a crisis happens, it's almost like they change their mode . . . they all mobilize together."

Boundary-spanning individuals

An equally powerful theme in this study was the presence of boundary-spanning individuals (building on the phraseology of Michael, 1973, and Finch, 1977), key school leaders who utilize numerous strategies and techniques to strengthen the comfort levels and understandings of adults in diverse professions. These individuals are adept at managing novel interdependencies among adults as their organizations become more complex (Finch, 1977, p. 298).

Three of the four principals in the study acted in this boundary-spanning role, as did seven of the eight SBHC coordinators (see Sloan, 1995). These three building administrators fit Goldring and Rallis's description (1993) of "principals-in-charge [who] accept the boundary-spanning function and proactively engage in managing the environment" (p. 71). They utilized numerous strategies to enhance adult understandings of collaborative services for children. One teacher commented, "It was hard in the beginning, because they [the SBHC staff] didn't have any idea how a school runs, and we didn't have any idea about medical models in schools. We both had a lot to learn." Another teacher commented, "You need someone like our principal, who keeps saying, 'What else can we do? Are we using it [the SBHC] effectively, or not? What are your gripes?'" Principals spoke of inviting health and human services professionals to faculty meetings and how this would facilitate the learning process between groups. A teacher explained: "There are a lot of boundaries, like the children's right to privacy. And we had a lot of difficulty with how they [the SBHC] could communicate with us and how we could communicate with them. We would send a child to the clinic, and we wouldn't know what happened. . . . [The principal] invited them to a couple of staff meetings. . . . It wasn't antagonistic. But we had to say, like, we really need to know. . . . After that, we all kind of collaborated."

Further comments from teachers yielded additional principal strategies: "Very often she will check something out for us in the SBHC, rather than burdening our special services staff, who's only here part-time. She's an exceptional leader." Candid comments also emerged at a school where teamwork would not have occurred without the principal "laying down the law" with two reportedly intransigent teachers. "She had to push them a little and said we are a team and you are going to have to learn how to do it." "Learning how to do it" translated into team-building workshops and "the formalization of teacher knowledge"—a strategy developed by the principal to strengthen understandings of what it is that health and human service professionals do and how that knowledge could assist teachers in facilitating student academic progress. A physician's assistant remarked, "The principal facilitated this formalization of knowledge about medical issues. I think everyone relies on her."

Individual principals discussed ways teachers and SBHC professionals could strengthen comfort levels between them right from the outset. They described what they had done when SBHCs were first introduced into their academic setting, describing logo contests, dedication ceremonies, welcome breakfasts, workshops, and articles about new staff (both teachers and SBHC professionals) in school newsletters. An SBHC coordinator related how one principal introduced new SBHC staff to teachers: "We toured the new staff person around, poked our noses collectively into every classroom in that building, introduced her, and said 'this is the new SBHC social worker.'" Another principal explained, "Whatever we do, we include them—medically, professionally, educationally, whatever—as much as possible. They are part of our family." Serious and extremely sensitive issues like confidentiality and referral processes were also mediated by boundary-spanning principals, who brought teachers and health and human services professionals to the table to discuss alternative methods of handling such issues. These key individuals helped adults collaborate creatively without violating confidentiality or compromising professional standards. Figure 4.1 outlines the many and varied leadership strategies utilized by principals, within the context of three developmental phases of SBHCs.

Implications for leadership in schools and communities

After reflecting for a moment on the themes in this study and boundary-spanning individuals' unique ways of creating bonds and partnerships among adults working with underserved children, one might ask, What can be recommended to schools and communities planning to initiate a collaborative service model? What should those responsible for such initiatives be expected to know? What should they do to help incorporate professionals who are traditionally from outside education into public school settings? How can administrators facilitate partnerships within the context of such a new phenomenon?

First and foremost, building administrators preparing to incorporate an SBHC or other collaborative services unit into their school must be cognizant of the dramatic change such an integration presents to the traditional public school. No longer will the school be an environment populated solely by educators, all imbued with professional commonalities. The introduction of health and human services agencies into schools suddenly merges together adults with strikingly different professional backgrounds. In all probability, most of these adults will not have worked in a public school setting before. Given these reflections and the diverse levels of SBHC integration at different sites (see Sloan, 1995), the importance of the leadership strategies of these key individuals cannot be underestimated.

Although the use of boundary-spanning strategies cannot guarantee that a collaborative work environment will develop, findings from this study do point to the presence of these strategies (or the lack thereof) as exerting an impact on teacher understandings and comfort levels. At one site, where the principal did not act as a boundary spanner, a negative mind-set persisted among many teachers. Participants voiced confusion about the concept of an SBHC and were uncomfortable with the presence of the health and human services professionals. The only teachers at this site who exhibited high comfort levels were those who interacted on their own with SBHC staff, a direct result of their students' personal involvement with the center. For various reasons, interactions between teachers and SBHC staff were neither fostered nor facilitated by the building administrator at this school.

Murphy (1992) encourages leadership preparation programs to think about ways to mesh the energies and efforts of various agencies working with educators in the school building. Ways to mesh these energies and develop partnerships was evidenced at the other three sites in the study, where administrators utilized boundary-spanning strategies that reached to the core of managerial and leadership issues. Teachers at these schools expressed a keen interest in the goals of the SBHC, understood the health and human services professionals' roles and responsibilities, and enjoyed learning to interact with the SBHC staff as a team. They clearly understood the need for all professionals to work collaboratively to meet children's multiple needs. Most importantly, teachers credited all of their understandings to principals who, in Foster's terms (1986), made sense of the diverse professional languages and communicated that understanding through various boundary-spanning strategies (p. 186). These principals "valued the actions . . . and language of [all] individuals in the organization" (p. 63) and, indeed, "provided the glue necessary to hold a school together . . . a good bit of each day [was spent] seeking to ensure, or at least negotiate, within-school cooperation" (Smylie, Crowson, Chou, and Levin, 1994, p. 349).

If we broaden the scope of our thinking about strategies and levels of integration and talk in terms of desired outcomes for children and how school leaders can facilitate them, the study's findings can be viewed in yet a different way. If we become trapped in a vacuum of extrapolated findings that simply discuss principals' strategies for strengthening collaboration and do not connect these findings to the overall welfare of children, the importance of this type of research is questionable. Knapp (1995) reminds us that "we may unwittingly become preoccupied with the intricacies of collaboration . . . and lose sight of the ends (e.g., children's health, education, and welfare)" (p. 15).

How do principals strengthen interdependencies, proactively heighten comfort levels, and perform boundary-spanning functions (Michael, 1973; Finch, 1977; Goldring and Rallis, 1993), all with the ultimate goal of strengthening all the facets of a child's education? In the reconstructionists' language, how can schools perform a regenerative function that actually reshapes the future for children and serves to relieve chronic social ills? Buttressed by the findings in this study, school leaders must take the ideas of boundary-spanning principals, as well as lessons gleaned from the power of the societal imperative, and view these within the context of strengthening the overall professional culture of the school.

Prior to learning and employing boundary-spanning strategies, it is imperative that principals

- Transcend their own professional canons of practice
- Believe in the concept of collaborative services as an efficient and

caring way to resolve the health, social, and academic problems of children and youth
- Learn the languages of different professional cultures
- Model collaborative behavior with teachers, parents, and other adult personnel

These should be viewed as stringent criteria for the subsequent (and then parallel) process of bringing diverse professions to the table for conversation. Principals are then better able to determine which steps and strategies are necessary to pave the way for schools and community agencies to introduce a health center into an educational environment, cooperate to implement the concept, continue to deal with sensitive issues, and work toward integrating the facility into the public school setting. Against the backdrop of these discussions, the principal should facilitate an empathic work environment. Adults interacting within the same setting, and with the same children, will then be better able to understand and empathize with each other's professional cultures, responsibilities, and perspectives on addressing children's needs. Figure 4.2 illustrates the vital role played by the principal in creating this healthy professional culture, a work environment that truly serves as a vehicle to connect the health, social, and academic components of children's lives.

Conclusion

In this study I listened to adults who work with children and youth describe their daily struggles to resolve medical, social, and academic problems. Driven by a societal imperative to meet the sometimes overwhelming needs of those in their care, the participants were greatly assisted by leaders who discovered commonalities across the problem areas and facilitated conversations and partnerships between and among different professionals.

Data from the study imply that the social ills of America's children are so serious and complex that collaborative services for children must be viewed within the context of long-term policy and practice. At one site in the study, teacher anxiety was extremely high due to funding cutbacks, which impacted SBHC services. Given the traditional short-term grants and funding offered most SBHCs in this country, professional anxiety becomes a greater likelihood. This is significant, because too often the sound philosophical basis for implementing collaborative services for children cannot save a program that becomes entangled and derailed at the level of the frontline professional.

The entire concept of collaborative services for children must be viewed from a community perspective, where needs, priorities, policy, and funding are taken into account on a larger, long-term scale and where the onus of responsibility is upon many others in leadership roles—researchers, funders, service providers, policymakers, community spokespersons, and educators—to institutionalize a philosophy of caring for children and youth. Meeting the complex needs of all children in this country cannot be accomplished with a few isolated conversations, a few effective administrators, or some unique partnerships among health, human services, and education professionals. In the words of John Dewey (1916), "The environment consists of the sum total of conditions . . . of all the activities of fellow beings that are bound up in the carrying on of the activities of any one of its members" (p. 22).

References

Clark, B. R. "Interorganizational Patterns in Education." *Administrative Science Quarterly*, 1965, *10*, 224–237.

Cortese, P. A. "Accomplishments in Comprehensive School Health Education." *Journal of School Health*, 1993, *63*(1), 21–23.

Cummings, T. G., and Worley, C. G. *Organizational Development and Change*. New York: West Publishing, 1993.

Dewey, J. *Democracy & Education*. London: Collier MacMillan, 1916.

Dryfoos, J. G. *Full-Service Schools: A Revolution in Health and Social Services for Children, Youth, and Families*. San Francisco: Jossey-Bass, 1994.

Finch, F. E. "Collaborative Leadership in Work Settings." *Journal of Applied Behavioral Science*, 1977, *13*(3), 292–302.

Foster, W. *Paradigms and Promises*. Amherst, N.Y.: Prometheus Books, 1986.

Goldring, E. B., and Rallis, S. F. *Principals of Dynamic Schools: Taking Charge of Change*. Thousand Oaks, Calif.: Corwin, 1993.

Hooper-Briar, L., and Lawson, H. A. *Serving Children, Youth and Families Through Interprofessional Collaboration and Service Integration: A Framework for Action*. Philadelphia: National Forum for the Danforth Foundation and the Institute for Educational Renewal at Miami University, 1994.

Jehl, J., and Kirst, M. "Getting Ready to Provide School-Linked Services: What Schools Must Do." In R. Behrman (ed.), *The Future of Children*. Los Altos, Calif.: Center for the Future of Children, 1992.

Kirby, D., and Lovick, S. "School-Based Health Clinics." *Educational Horizons*, 1987, *5*(3), 139–143.

Knapp, M. S. "How Shall We Study Comprehensive, Collaborative Services for Children and Families?" *Educational Researcher*, 1995, *24*(4), 5–16.

Michael, D. N. *On Learning to Plan and Planning to Learn*. San Francisco: Jossey-Bass, 1973.

Murphy, J. *The Landscape of Leadership Preparation*. Thousand Oaks, Calif.: Corwin, 1992.

Portner, J. "An Ounce of Prevention." *Education Week*, February 2, 1994, pp. 18–22.

Sloan, E. S. "In the Name of the Child: An Exploratory Multi-Case Study of Collaborative Interactions in Elementary School-Based Health Centers in Connecticut." Unpublished doctoral dissertation, the University of Connecticut, 1995.

Smylie, M. A., Crowson, R. L., Chou, V., and Levin, R. A. "The Principal and Community–School Connections in Chicago's Radical Reform." *Education Administration Quarterly*, 1994, *30*(3), 342–364.

Trist, E .L. "Collaborations in Work Settings." *The Journal of Applied Behavioral Science*, 1977, *13*(3), 268–278.

Tyack, D. "Health and Social Services in Public Schools: Historical Perspectives." In R. Behrman (ed.), *The Future of Children*. Los Altos, Calif.: Center for the Future of Children, 1992.

Waszak, C., and Neidell, S. *School-Based and School-Linked Clinics: Update 1991*. Washington, D.C.: Center for Population Options, Support Center for School-Based Health Centers, 1991.

Zigler, E. F., Kagan, S. L., and Klugman, E. *Children, Families, and Government*. Cambridge, England: Cambridge University Press, 1983.

ELLEN SMITH SLOAN *is assistant professor of education, University of Connecticut School of Education, Department of Educational Leadership, Storrs, Connecticut.*

This case study of a successful writer-in-residence program examines the intrinsic motivation supplied by using the writing process as part of a larger classroom dialogue, along with the tensions that arise when members of an artistic community that puts a high value on self-expression forms a partnership in the highly structured environment of a public school.

5

Using the arts to integrate knowledge: Partnerships between schools and nonprofit organizations

Liane Brouillette

The evidence that U.S. public schools are not working well is depressingly familiar. One in five young Americans drops out of high school. Nearly half of all high school graduates have not mastered seventh-grade arithmetic. American 13-year-olds place near the bottom in science and math achievement in international comparisons. One-third of 17-year-olds cannot place France on a map of the world. . . .

Of even greater concern, perhaps, is that many schools have wavered from liberal educational purposes. They are hunkered down instead in a short-sighted utilitarianism that leaves little room for the free play of young people's curiosity, respect for knowledge as a good in itself, and the cultivation of the imagination and the sense of beauty.

Benno Schmidt, 1992, p. A12.

THIS BLEAK ASSESSMENT by a former president of Yale University succinctly summarizes the viewpoint of many Americans who have

NEW DIRECTIONS FOR SCHOOL LEADERSHIP, NO. 2, WINTER 1996 © JOSSEY-BASS PUBLISHERS

lost faith in the ability of our public schools to cope with challenges the nation now faces. Studies that underline the severity of the problem are not difficult to find. According to *Adult Literacy in America*, a 1993 report from the National Center for Education Statistics, nearly half of adult Americans are barely literate, possessing such limited reading and writing skills that they cannot perform simple tasks like writing a letter explaining a billing error (Henry, 1993; Gage, 1992).

In the face of such criticisms, educators rightly point to the concerted attempts that have been made to meet the problem of declining educational performance head-on. Joseph Murphy says of the 1980s school reform movement, "The attack on a host of identified problems and deficiencies has been more comprehensive, directed more at the general student population (and less at targeted groups), of greater concentrated intensity, and has spawned more activity than at any time in the past. The reform agenda also has been sustained longer than previous efforts, actually shifting into a second generation or wave of change" (1990, pp. 5–6). Yet, state and federal initiatives have often been generated with little regard for their interrelationship or their cumulative local effects (Kimbrough and Hill, 1981; Kirst, 1988; Wise, 1979). Some of the reforms mandated by the federal and state governments have also become problematic in that they focus on raising standardized test scores at the expense of programs that might encourage the "free play of young people's curiosity."

But how do schools avoid becoming "hunkered down in a short-sighted utilitarianism"? School people have only so much time and energy. Often, the drill and repetition required to help all students score at a minimum level on competency tests leaves little time for the "cultivation of imagination and the sense of beauty." After a day of setting out rules and pointing out right ways and wrong ways, it is difficult to shift gears and move into the kind of imaginative romps that lay at the root of creativity. Several inner-city teachers I interviewed for this study commented that they frequently felt as much in need of a breath of intellectual fresh air as did their students. These teachers were involved in long-term partnerships (usually twenty-six weeks) with professional writers working in the public schools. The writers were associated with Writers in the Schools (WITS), a nonprofit organization in Houston, Texas, that has placed writers in more than 450 such year-long residencies.

The study

Programs that bring poets, dramatists, and fiction writers into the schools to interact with children have become a popular way of providing students with direct exposure to the literary arts. However, although there is substantial anecdotal evidence that children become more enthusiastic writers under the long-term tutelage of a writer-in-residence, few attempts have been made to systematically observe how experienced writers-in-residence interact with students or to analyze how their techniques differ from traditional classroom practice.

This chapter summarizes a year-long ethnographic study of a partnership between a large urban school district and a nonprofit organization that during the 1993–94 school year placed professional writers in over fifty long-term, in-school residencies. Writers visited three classrooms weekly for one hour each. The objective of the study was to observe respected classroom teachers and professional writers as they taught writing to students. A special focus was the unspoken assumptions about the role and purpose of writing that grew out of the school and literary cultures. Of particular interest was the manner in which the teaching approaches used by the professional writers differed from the writing process approach used in the classrooms of most participating teachers.

Twelve long-term partnerships between writers-in-residence and classroom teachers were investigated during the course of this year-long study. Classroom observations were carried out. All teacher-writer pairs in the study worked in the inner-city schools in the Houston Independent School District (HISD), which educates two hundred thousand students of diverse ethnicity (46 percent Hispanic, 37 percent African American, 14 percent Anglo, 3 percent Asian).

A Blending of cultures

Complex cultural and pedagogical issues arise when members of an artistic community that puts a high value on self-expression enter a highly structured environment such as an urban public school. From the beginning of the present study it was clear that the role of "writer as artist" put forward by writers-in-residence working in public schools contrasted in significant ways with the way the role of "student writer" was constructed in these classrooms during the remainder of the week. An African American writer with extensive experience working with urban children explained how he structured the writing experience for children he worked with:

What I feel I bring, as a writer, is a fresh approach, even in the words I use to describe familiar terms. For example, my third-graders get a kick out of defining a paragraph as a family of sentences, or rap as a poem with a beat, or elaboration as stre-e-e-e-tching a sentence. In my class we define *why* not as the beginning of "Why do I have to do this . . . ?" but as the word that makes us dig a little deeper. And the shovel we use is the word *because*. When I have children start building up a homemade thesaurus, I call it "building ammunition."

Children like a fresh approach, but they also value having little rituals they can depend on. Even the moment when I have to take my leave has its own little ritual, which eases the leave-taking. I say, "Got to leave now," and the class echoes back, "Peace!"

Viewing writing as organic

Although the writers often brought classic and contemporary literature into classrooms, they operated from the assumption that it was through sharing and discussing their own writing that students were most inspired. Children working with a writer-in-residence were taught that writing is an ongoing process, beginning with the seed that is the original idea and growing, through additional ideas and through the feedback of others, into a finished work. As one classroom teacher put it, "The writer encourages the children to trust their own perceptions, to write in their own voices, and then to make the changes that allow people to comprehend as *they* comprehend."

A primary goal of the writer-in-residence program was that of helping to awaken in inner-city children a delight in and appreciation for the written word. The goal was to transform their attitude toward what many students had come to consider the drudgery of writing. Assumptions expressed by participating writers included the following:

- Playfulness lies at the heart of all creative work.
- The opportunity to give free rein to the imagination is central to student engagement in the writing process.
- Writing and thinking are closely related.
- Writing provides children with the tools to understand their lives and to become active shapers of their experience.
- The arts nourish each other; the visual arts, drama, music, dance, and photography can be powerful spurs to writing, and vice versa.
- Each writer-in-residence works best from the wellspring of his or her own creative process, designing lessons in response to needs of particular students and teachers.
- Teachers need to actively pursue their own writing in order to understand and support the writer's work in their classrooms.

Tensions sometimes arose between teachers and writers, based on the differing values each placed on playfulness and order as part of the classroom culture. However, writers' attitudes were, in several cases, modified as the year progressed, and the newness of having a writer in the classroom wore off. As the writer became a more familiar figure, some children began testing limits. Writers began to comment upon the connection between writing and teaching: "Just as you feel vulnerable when you [stand up to] read your creative writing to a group, teaching is very personal. Just as in writing, you can't really hide who you are when you teach." Writers' comments about most teachers became more admiring as the year progressed.

As partners, writers tended to value teachers when they had already created a culture conducive to writing, regularly gave children time for writing, had classroom management skills that made discipline all but invisible, and had faith in the writer, even if the writer did something unexpected.

Teacher expectations of writers

Although it had been made clear at the beginning of the residencies that the writers would not teach to the high-stakes standardized tests administered yearly throughout the state of Texas, it was clear that many teachers and principals hoped that bringing a writer into the classroom would help to enhance student scores on the written portion of these tests. At times this unspoken expectation created palpable tensions, such as when writers told students to just keep writing, without stopping to check spelling or correct grammar, during freewriting exercises or when only a few rough drafts were chosen for extensive revision. Teachers who were accustomed to bringing the writing process full circle tended to find it unsettling when writers allowed students to set aside nearly finished pieces they were not satisfied with and start again. On the other hand, several teachers expressed pleasure that "the kids will at least have this one chance each week to write for writing's sake."

Classroom teachers' initial expectations in regard to the writer-in-residence who would be working with them included that the writer

- Possess a great deal of knowledge about writing
- Have a passion for literary art
- Be able to adapt to the culture of the classroom
- Be able to effectively communicate with children
- Be able to connect effectively with each individual child

The first four of these expectations were easily fulfilled. Most of the writers-in-residence were pursuing graduate degrees in creative writing. Not all of them made a strong and immediate connection with the children in their classes, however.

Many of the writers had little experience dealing with children in a classroom situation. They needed teacher assistance in understanding the classroom culture and learning to express abstract ideas in a manner children could easily understand. At times, the writers' dependence on teachers' classroom management skills became problematic, such as when the free and easy give-and-take that writers encouraged among students conflicted with the established culture of the classroom. When children got too excited and the teacher reacted sternly, the mood of exuberant spontaneity the writer had attempted to nurture was also dampened.

On the other hand, teachers were greatly pleased to discover that, in addition to their expertise in creative writing, some of the writers also brought with them a knowledge of a minority or international culture. The extra dimension that such writers could bring to the classroom is exemplified in the following field notes excerpt:

All but four of the two dozen first-graders in this ESL class are native Urdu speakers. Two are Somali. Since S. is from Pakistan, the country of origin of the parents of most of these students, many of them greeted her excitedly in Urdu when she entered, or broke into Urdu when they became excited, either during the lesson or while dictating their stories to S. toward the end of the hour. Some of the children had very limited knowledge of English.

The class started with S. reading aloud some of the notes that had been written to her on a day when the teacher was absent due to sickness and the lesson plan had suggested that the substitute teacher have the children use their language arts period to write notes to S. The children beamed as their notes were read.

The teacher-writer relationship

Since the writers—who only visited a specific classroom for one hour a week—could only work within the system already established by the teacher, their authority was grounded in the teacher's authority, which had to be "borrowed" by the writers, especially at the beginning of the year. One writer described her relationship to the class as something like that of a stepparent: "These are not your children; they are your partner's—in this case, the classroom teacher's. You must therefore have a healthy relationship with the teacher. Only when a teacher asks you into her room and understands or at least supports your presence will you reach his or her children." Possibilities for misunderstanding were ever-present. As one writer noted, "Having someone walk into your classroom (as writers do to classroom teachers) can be intrusive. Or having someone watch you teach (which the teacher does each time the writer teaches) can be threatening as well. So we have to work hard to set up a situation in which writer and teacher aren't standing at opposite sides of the classroom, threatened by one another."

Had it been possible, prior to the beginning of the school year, to provide staff development opportunities to allow teachers to experience writing exercises similar to those writers-in-residence would later use with their students, and to discuss their reactions, some of these tensions may have been avoided. During the period of this study, a voluntary eleven-week writing seminar for teachers involved with the program was held by Dr. Marv Hoffman at Rice University. The hands-on experience with the writing process that teachers gained through this workshop appeared to break down cultural barriers between writers and teachers, allowing a cross-fertilization of expertise. Teachers who participated in the workshop reported having a good rapport with their writers-in-residence, as well as enhanced student learning.

What we can learn

When writers entered a school where little writing was happening or writing was limited to preparing for high-stakes standardized tests, their mission was relatively clear and their impact was often dramatic and immediate. Where teachers became enthusiastic about writing themselves and were armed with sophisticated ideas, activities, structures, and assessment techniques, lasting changes were made in classroom practice and culture. A few teachers made arrangements with their schools that enabled them first to observe writers' lessons in their own classrooms and then, through creative scheduling, replicate those sessions in other classrooms, thus sharing them with other teachers in addition to incorporating those lessons into their own permanent repertoire. In such schools, the writers' visits became more than isolated events taking place in a few classrooms. No longer just a private performance done by students for a sole teacher to critique, student writing became a community event, part of a broader dialogue.

Teachers who themselves did little writing beyond required school paperwork tended to ritualize the writing process by spelling out the steps and requiring students to go through all of them for every piece of writing. In contrast, writers-in-residence emphasized looking at models of what good writing looked like and using varied forms to teach specific skills. For example, Haiku helped students learn to cut out excess words by sharpening their awareness of how just a few carefully chosen words can have great power. Descriptive narrative taught them effective use of adjectives. Playwriting imparted an awareness of the rhythms of dialogue. Those teachers who became committed to expanding their approach to the writing process were able to expand upon the new awareness created by these exercises and to help students generalize their new skills to other kinds of writing.

The teachers who proved most successful in helping students achieve this synthesis were those who made a regular practice of writing along with their students, often using the writing process as part of a larger classroom dialogue that allowed students to bring their home experiences into the schoolroom through reading their work out loud, as in this example: "I'm going to tell you a story about me. Every time I go to my great-grandma's house after school, I walk in and throw my backpack on the floor because I am glad when school's out. I go and sit by my great-grandma and when I hug her I feel like I can feel her bones and her heart." In such instances as this, student writing serves not only as a demonstration of a certain set of skills but also as an expression of the child's individuality, a chance for the reader to see the world through the child's eyes.

In those classrooms where teacher-writer collaborations proved most successful, the interplay between the writing process approach used by the teachers and the task-specific approach adopted by the writers resulted in both teacher and writer putting increased emphasis on the function of writing as an instrument of human communication. Significant informal staff development opportunities came about where teachers with writers in their classrooms were encouraged to meet regularly and share creative new ideas with teachers who did not have a writer-in-residence. Dialogue about writing progressed toward deciding how a particular image or idea could be effectively communicated to the reader—with the student writer allowed to stand as the final authority on whether his or her vision had been given suitable written form. In sharing their stories, children became part of a coherent classroom culture where each child's story was known and formed part of a larger whole.

Helping children integrate knowledge

Several respondents in this study justified partnerships between writers and visual artists or writers and musicians on the grounds that the arts nourish one another. Given the differences between arts-based collaborations and much pedagogical practice in the public schools, such a statement may mean little to the reader. One way to make the meaning clearer is to allow the reader to "witness" a lesson. The following field notes excerpt describes a lesson that took place during a WITS field trip to the Community Music Center of Houston, where Samuel Dinkins III presented a workshop entitled "Rap, Rhythm, and Rhyme" to approximately ninety African American third-graders. Students not only learned about African culture and the African roots of contemporary U.S. rap music but had the opportunity to read their own previously written poems to the beat of African drums. Not only was this lesson highly informative, but by demonstrating the process by which a poem can become a song, it helped students integrate their knowledge of writing with their interest in contemporary music.

This collaboration of writer and musician modeled for the students the complex cultural processes by which the rhythms of Africa and the ruminations of contemporary American youth have become joined in the musical genre known as rap. Sam Dinkins is the speaker:

Your writer has been teaching you about poetry and how to write. A lot of what you have written could be put to music and made into a song. What you are going to learn about today is how you could go about doing that.

Does anyone take music in school? What do you take? [Two children take piano, one takes drums, and a dozen are in choir.] That's great! What does *percussion* mean? [Children look puzzled.] Think of brass instruments. They are made of brass. And woodwinds used to be made of wood. What about percussion instruments? ["You hit them?"] Yes! Stand right up here and say that real loud to everyone. [Laughter. "You hit them!"]

Percussion means anything you strike or hit. When you clap your hands, that's percussion. A piano is a percussion instrument, one that has "definite pitch." Any instrument that can be tuned to the notes A B C D E F G has definite pitch. The kalemba or thumb piano is an African instrument with definite pitch. [Sam shows kalemba to children and plays a tune.]

See those drums in the back of the room? They are kettle drums of timpani. [He plays a scale on the drums.] This has definite pitch. [Children laugh, surprised that anyone could play a scale on a drum.]

Non–definite pitch instruments are like this tambourine. [Shakes.] Or these maracas. Where do maracas come from? ["Mexico!"] There's another instrument that the maracas were derived from. This comes from Africa. It's called a shekari. It used to be a plant, a squash. [Passes it to child.] Hold it gently. Look on the inside and pass it down. They took all the food out and ate it. Then they left it in the sun, and it dried out and they used it to carry water in. A calabash. Then they put beads on the outside and it became an instrument, a shekari. [He plays a rhythm by shaking it.] Is it definite pitch, or non–definite pitch? ["Non–definite pitch!"] So, you see, the shekari is like maracas, except the beads are on the outside. With the maracas they're on the inside.

What's this? ["A cowbell!"] Here's another one from the cowbell family, a go-go bell. It has two tones. It's derived from an African instrument.

These are West African bells, gongagway bells. [Plays double bell, which is struck from the outside.] *Autophonic* is the word we use for instruments made out of metal or wood. Other percussion instruments are made from membranes.

This one looks like little sticks. It's called "klaves." In Spanish that means "little sticks." These are very important to Latin music because the klave player keeps everyone together. Remember, when it's time to play the instruments, you can't play what you can't name!

This is a talking drum from Africa. [Holds up a drum with woven cords attached to the outside and plays it, squeezing or slacking up on the cords on the outside to raise or lower the pitch.] This drum works the same way your vocal cords do. Women talk in higher voices because their vocal cords are shorter. Men's are longer, so their voices are lower. The best drummers in the world come from the West Coast of Africa. Give me a sentence. [He is handed a child's notebook and plays the drum, reading a sentence aloud at the same time. The intonation of the drum and that of the voice are remarkably similar.]

Human beings were made rhythmic. Your heart has a beat. So does your breath. The way you walk or run or move your hands is based on rhythm. Notice how your eyes blink. They blink in the pattern of your heartbeat. [Imitates heartbeat on drum, first slowly, then as if after running. Children giggle and clap when he's done.] Don't forget. You're very rhythmic.

See? When you squeeze real tight, it tightens the drumhead. When you let it loose, it loosens the drumhead. The drumhead is made out of goat skin. The strings are goat hair, and the wood is teak.

These instruments over here are hand drums. [Plays on a set of drums.] The large drum is a tomba. Say "tomba." ["Tomba."] Konga is the middle drum. ["Konga."] Quinto is the smallest. ["Quinto."] In Africa they're the papa drum, the mama drum, and the baby drum. Bongo is both these two drums here. They're *not* called "bongos" with an *s*. Both together are "the bongo." [Plays.] Notice all the finger movement. There are five distinct notes you can play on all of these drums: bass, tone, rim, slap, and a muffle note. [Demonstrates.]

[Children sway to the rhythm as he goes back and plays an assortment of the instruments he has introduced, with tape-recorded drum rhythms in the background. They clap loudly when he finishes.] I had two drum patterns going on under what I was doing. That's what rap is. It's called sampling, putting a sample of one thing over another. There's nothing new musically under the sun, just different versions and ways of putting things together.

Who was the first modern rapper? I say "modern" because they had rappers in Africa. They were called griots, or storytellers. Remember, everyone stands on everyone else's shoulders. Take a listen. [Plays tape.] Those people were called the Last Poets, and the song was "On the Subway." That's traditional rap. They're using acoustic instruments, and they were using their voices to imitate the subway. There were no electronics. "Rappers Delight" by the Sugar Hill Gang was the first modern rap song.

Another style of rap sounds like talking. Modern rap is real syncopated, in time with the beat. Who are your favorite rappers? [Children call out names too quickly to write down.] You guys need to listen to more positive rap!

A boy is invited up to play the drum set. Sam demonstrates a simple rhythm using the bass, snare, and cymbal. The boy plays, while the other children grin and watch intently. "Who's a good reader?" A girl comes up and reads a poem, while the boy on the drums provides a background beat.

Conclusion

This case study of a successful writer-in-residence program explored how, through creating partnerships between schools and nonprofit agencies, educators can nurture a climate that encourages the free play of young people's curiosity, a respect for knowledge as a good in itself, and the cultivation of meaningful dialogue among members of the school community. The teacher-writer relationship emphasized the trust, readiness, and common agenda needed by all involved in the partnership.

Arts-based partnerships can help extend the vision of school personnel beyond that of short-sighted utilitarianism, which so often results from a combination of severe budget restraints and increased pressure to produce high scores on standardized tests. However, careful planning is needed if misunderstandings are to be avoided when members of an artistic community that puts a high value on self-expression enter the highly structured environment of a public school. Both initial orientation and ongoing staff development are needed to assist teachers in thinking through the leadership issues that arise when traditional boundaries are crossed or merged.

References

Gage, R."If U Cn Reed Thiz Storie." *U.S. News & World Report*, June 5, 1992, p. 10.

Henry, T. "90 Million Can Barely Read, Write." *USA Today*, Sept. 9, 1993, p. 1A.

Kimbrough, J., and Hill, P. *The Aggregate Effects of Federal Education Programs.* Santa Monica, Calif.: Rand Corp., 1981.

Kirst, M. W. *Who Should Control Our Schools: Reassessing Current Policies.* Stanford, Calif.: Center for Education Research, 1988.

Murphy, J. "The Educational Reform Movement of the 1980s: A Comprehensive Analysis." In J. Murphy (ed.), *The Educational Reform Movement of the 1980s.* Berkeley, Calif.: McCutchan, 1990.

National Center for Education Statistics. *Adult Literacy in America.* Washington, D.C.: National Center for Education Statistics, 1993.

Schmidt, B. C. "Educational Innovation for Profit," *Wall Street Journal,*, 1992, p. A12.

U.S. News & World Report. 1993, Sept. 20.

Wise, A. *Legislated Learning.* Berkeley: University of California Press, 1979.

LIANE BROUILLETTE *is assistant professor at the University of Houston in the department of educational leadership and cultural studies.*

This chapter describes several partnerships between schools and religious organizations and examines the potentially powerful role they can play together.

6

The potential for partnerships between schools and religious organizations

Richard D. Lakes, Paula A. Cordeiro

A MAIN GOAL OF EDUCATIONAL PARTNERSHIPS is to support and enhance learning opportunities for youth. Marshaling all the potential resources in a community is crucial when addressing children's needs, and religious organizations are some of the most prominent of community assets. Formal partnerships between schools and churches offer much potential, yet few examples exist of long-term partnerships of this type.

The vast potential of having religious organizations work with schools remains relatively untapped primarily due to differing concerns regarding the separation of church and state. Too many educators have been confused by the notion that any kind of partnership with a religious organization means crossing forbidden boundaries. Without teaching or promoting religion, public education can effectively partner with churches. Irrespective of the specific religious faith—Christian, Judaic, Buddhist, Islamic, and so on—tapping the assets of religious organizations by partnering with them offers great potential for helping communities address the social, economic, educational, and spiritual needs of their children.

NEW DIRECTIONS FOR SCHOOL LEADERSHIP, NO. 2, WINTER 1996 © JOSSEY-BASS PUBLISHERS

In this chapter we argue that excluding religious organizations from the list of potential community partners for local schools amounts to ignoring one of the most powerful assets that every community possesses. First we explore the historic reasons for the dearth of partnerships between schools and religious organizations. Next, we describe several examples of recently developed partnerships between schools and religious organizations. Finally, using the example of a current faith-based community outreach program, we detail strategies that educators can use to access and enhance the effectiveness of community programs offered by churches.

A brief overview of schools and their religious ties

As early as 1647, "Townships with a hundred or more household-ers were required to establish a Latin grammar school" that had as the main curriculum objective "to produce God-fearing Christians" (Tanner and Tanner, 1990, p. 31). Religious indoctrination was of paramount importance in these early schools. Schooling was con-sidered God's work (Tyack, 1967). The teacher was "almost-but-not-quite a minister" (Lortie, 1975, p. 11). Teachers taught Bible lessons, which were an important part of every school day. Calvin-ism and the Church of England shaped views on education, and "the predominant objective and spirit of education was religious" (Tanner and Tanner, 1990, p. 36). The idea was that education was synonymous with salvation.

Throughout the 1880s, as the religious diversity of the nation increased, controversies emerged regarding which version of the Bible should be used in schools (for example, Catholics objected to Protestant versions of the Bible). Many immigrants were repelled by the domination of Protestants in public schools, and this led to a growing number of parochial schools.

During the twentieth century, several landmark court cases sig-nificantly altered religious ties with schools. Although some have argued that the decision in the 1927 *Scopes* v. *Tennessee* case was a defeat for fundamentalism because it allowed evolution to be taught in schools, others view the reaction to this case as the impetus for fundamentalists to rally and strengthen their enrollments. By the 1960s, Christian fundamentalism began to flourish. Conflicts increased between fundamentalists and more mainstream Christians due to the tactics employed by fundamentalists in schools as well as with other institutions. Court cases and controversies over textbooks, concepts such as evolution, multicultural education, and sex education became widespread.

Due to these controversies, supplemented by the legal ramifications of the First Amendment, educators are reluctant to form partnerships with churches. Two clauses of the First Amendment have led to misunderstandings among the general population and to considerable controversy in the courts. Part of the First Amendment reads, "Congress shall make no law respecting an establishment of religion, or prohibiting the free exercise thereof." The establishment clause ("Congress shall make no law respecting an establishment of religion") promotes religious freedom by what the courts refer to as "separation." The free exercise clause ("or prohibiting the free exercise thereof") promotes freedom of religion by what is referred to as the "accommodation" principle. According to Nowak and Rotunda (1991), "there is a natural antagonism between a command not to establish religion and a command not to inhibit its practice" (p. 17). Thus, with the rise in power of fundamentalist Christians and the dichotomy between practicing religion and not practicing religion, most public schools have chosen to shun all controversy by avoiding any formalized relationships with churches. Just as our laws regarding tort reform have changed based on practical considerations viewed in light of the times, these clauses of the First Amendment are now being reinterpreted in view of contemporary needs and sentiments.

The majority of educators are beginning to realize that, although it is not appropriate for schools to teach religion, a legitimate role for schools is to teach *about* religion. As the controversy over values rages in U.S. institutions, professionals are recognizing that dialogue instead of debate is far more likely to help us achieve common understanding. As demands to address the multiple needs of all children are placed at the schoolhouse door, educators are beginning to reach out to community resources. One of the potentially most powerful of these resources is the human and sociocultural capital available in churches, mosques, temples, meetinghouses, and synagogues.

Religious diversity

One reason educational institutions may want to tap the assets of churches is the growing religious diversity of the United States. In 1990 Hill estimated that the United States had more than six million Muslims. Islam has surpassed Judaism as the number-two religion in the country, and Muslims outnumber Episcopalians by two to one. "Over the last 20 years Oklahoma City has acquired five mosques, four Hindu temples, one Sikh gurudwara, and three Buddhist temples (Eck, 1993, p. 99). Additionally, due to immigration from Asia, the ranks of religions such as Buddhism, Taoism, and Hinduism are increasing in the United States. Each of these religions brings different traditions, values, and beliefs. If schools are encouraged to partner with faith-based people and organizations, then children will feel more comfortable sharing and discussing their ideas and beliefs in the classroom. To argue that the home or religious institutions have sole responsibility for teaching values is nonsensical. Schools and teachers teach values every day, whether deliberately or unconsciously.

Perhaps a story will help illuminate this point. When one of the authors of this chapter was the principal of an American school in Spain, she invited a clergyman from a local Korean church to address the children in assembly about some of the new theater and arts classes his church was sponsoring. These programs were open to all children, regardless of their religion. Afterwards, one Korean student commented that he could not believe his eyes when he saw the clergyman get up to address the student body. He said that in all his years in American schools, he had never thought that any people from his faith would be welcome.

This example illustrates how children are often forced to compartmentalize their lives. Compartmentalized institutions do not serve children well, however. It makes no sense to force educational systems to work independently of one another, to have schools address students' academic learning from 8:00 to 3:00 and churches teach them values on Friday evening or Sunday morning. Instead, as educators begin to realize that schools are only one part of a larger educational system, it becomes apparent that tapping the resources of nearby components of that system is not only logical but mandatory.

Values, beliefs, and educational achievement

Another reason educational institutions must tap the assets of churches is the growing body of data supporting links between academic achievement and values and beliefs. Research has shown that religious affiliation and participation among children and youths tends to have a positive effect on adolescent behavior, minimizing high-risk practices such as substance abuse and sexual activity and limiting delinquency (see Mincy, 1994).

In researching academic achievement in the African American community, Janice Hale-Benson argued that "Black child-rearing has a strong religious orientation" (1986, p. 52). She found that the church plays a significant role in the lives of many African American families. According to Lynch and Hanson (1992) the African American church is the main place where community members learn the values and responsibilities of leadership and organizational skills. Although researchers have found that these churches are not as influential today as they were in the past, nevertheless, "the spiritual resources of the community have had a direct impact on the lives of most African American people of substance" (Lynch and Hanson, 1992, p. 136).

Caplan, Choy, and Whitmore (1991), in a major study of the academic success of refugees from Southeast Asia, found that cultural values played a significant role in the academic success of children. They report that in the case of Southeast Asians these values are tied to Confucian philosophy and the Buddhist faith. "These refugees brought with them a mixture of Buddhist and Confucian values and traditions that have provided a source of motivation and guidance with which to steer a successful course for their lives in America" (p. 139). The authors conclude that one of the main implications of their study is "the need to recognize the potential of the family and its culture to promote and produce achievement in its children" (p. 155). Cordeiro, Reagan, and Martinez (1994) state that key elements composing cultural identity are values and religious beliefs. Since the research literature provides ample evidence that there is a "fundamental and overriding effect of family life and basic values on achievement" (p. 159), then partnering with churches is an important link in filling gaps that may exist if family life does not offer children these values.

Churches and the community

In the past, churches have recognized the need to reach out to children and adolescents in more widespread ways than through religion classes. Since the 1940s, the Catholic church has launched a number of initiatives targeted at curtailing Latino youth gang membership (aside from its recreational offerings through Catholic Youth Organization sports leagues); the most successful of these efforts combine moral training with a social justice agenda for teenagers at weekend retreats (Stevens-Arroyo and Diaz-Stevens, 1993). The nondenominational Youth for Christ (YFC), begun in 1944, is very active in African American and Latino gang interventions through some of its 235 local chapters (Maxwell, 1994).

Another powerful example of activism and ministry was The Woodlawn Organization (TWO), established in Chicago in 1959 by an interdenominational alliance of four pastors concerned about the future of their community (Brazier, 1969; Fish, 1973). In a decade-long struggle, TWO obtained funding for a Head Start program, contracted with local industries for job training for the neighborhood unemployed, began an experimental schools project, and participated in the Model Cities program, planning development for proposed social service agencies and low-income housing units. This activist ministry considered youth development an important component of its overall agenda for community and economic justice.

In recent years there has been considerable interest on the part of churches in expanding their offerings to include the educational development of children. This has come to the attention of religious leaders throughout the nation, particularly those in urban environments. Challenges for religious leaders involve coordinating services with schools and other organizations, avoiding duplication of services, and eliminating gaps in educational programming. In the next section we describe three recently formulated school-linked partnerships that have the potential to address the educational, emotional, social, and spiritual needs of children more fully.

The Garden

The Garden of Prayer Baptist Church is an African American urban church located in the Montebello Waverly area of Baltimore, which, like many inner-city neighborhoods, has experienced dramatic increases in teen pregnancy, violence, drug use, and gangs. Local schools continue to report rising dropout rates. Recognizing that these needs had to be addressed, the congregation of the Garden repositioned themselves "as sources of secular as well as spiritual succor" (Drennan, 1996 p. 35). Besides operating a food pantry, distributing clothes in winter, and sponsoring a variety of health-related activities, the church began education programs for children and adolescents. The Garden has a reading center that offers Saturday morning literacy classes and individual attention, coordinated with local schools. Creating a partnership infrastructure that will ensure the quality and continuity of these programs is an ongoing challenge for local schools.

One Church/One School partnerships

One Church/One School is another type of partnership between schools and churches. Launched in 1991 in Chicago, this national initiative can now be found in Dallas, Chicago, Cleveland, and Gary, Indiana. In these partnerships, pastors are paired with school principals "to identify ways in which their churches could help out the schools" (Drennan, 1996, p. 36). Each partnership is unique to the school and addresses the specific needs of the community's children, with the church supplying resources and staffing (p. 36).

Cincinnati's Alternative Learning Centers

Another example of partnership between churches and schools is the six Alternative Learning Centers linked to schools in Cincinnati. Staffed by church volunteers and supported by the city's Baptist ministers, these centers provide resources for suspended and expelled students. Enrollment in the centers is voluntary, but parents must be involved in the decision. As many as sixty students attend the centers on any given school day, with students ranging from the first through twelfth grades. Since the centers have been successful in attracting children from the streets, monies have been donated by local businesses. In 1997 the ministers plan to expand the centers' offerings and open the Project Succeed Academy, designed to target suspended and expelled students.

These three partnership programs are still in their infancy; their full potential is still unknown. Partnerships such as these have the capacity to better integrate the various systems that make up children's lives.

Moving in the Spirit

Moving in the Spirit (MITS), a division of Family Services Consultation (FSC) Urban Ministries of Atlanta, is a notable faith-based organization that combines the educational and the spiritual. It is loosely linked with Atlanta's schools and emphasizes youth outreach. It was established in 1986 as a nonprofit organization to provide much-needed guidance to youth in Atlanta's inner-city shelters, schools, housing projects, and community centers. The major purpose of its programs is to teach workplace values and to empower young people to become self-reliant by focusing on respect, discipline, commitment, responsibility, and accountability through the application of traditional business procedures to the dance experience. This process enables youths to channel their creative and physical talents into positive experiences that cross over to other aspects of their lives such as family, education, spirituality, and future employment.

According to MITS cofounder and executive director Dana Marschalk, MITS offers four programs and outreach services for school-aged youths: Stepping Stones, The Apprentice Corporation, The Performance Company, and The Resource Network.[1] Stepping Stones' curriculum consists of dance fundamentals as well as social skills development. The teachers in this program are required to keep a notebook to track the progress of their kids, monitor the incentive system for point accrual, record a daily journal entry with reflections on their students and classes, and update or revise their lesson plans. There are two performances annually: an informal recital of works-in-progress and a Literacy in Motion recital in which books, poems, speeches, or stories chosen by the students are set to dance.

The Apprentice Corporation is an advanced program for teen dancers (some have participated in the Stepping Stones program). Membership is by yearly audition, and classes emphasize problem solving and creativity. There are twelve dancers in the company, a multiracial, multiethnic mix of inner-city boys and girls who perform in public spaces in the city as well as in summer venues throughout the United States.

The Performance Company is another program offered by MITS. It is a multicultural and intergenerational professional modern dance ensemble that addresses issues of urban culture and social justice. They produce two major productions each year and are featured at local cultural events in Atlanta. These dancers serve as role models for young participants in MITS and are available to share their talents with school arts programs.

The fourth program offered by MITS is the Resource Network, which coordinates volunteers, instructors, mentors, and workshop leaders as support for young participants in MITS programs. The Network's mission is accomplished through counseling and training in the areas of career opportunities, public speaking, alcohol and drug abuse, AIDS education, and teen pregnancy prevention.

MITS offers youths opportunities to explore their creative energies through visual projects that originate from the experiences of each participant. This dance ministry helps at-risk youths seek empowerment through performance art that gives voice to their lived experiences. The arts are democratizing influences for inner-city youths—reaching outward to new communities of individuals engaged in the creative process and to new venues for attracting audiences interested in these forms of cultural expression. Youths react positively when they realize that their aesthetic work is legitimized in public spaces—as murals on street corner buildings, sculpture in transportation centers, or performance pieces in public parks (see Heath and McLaughlin, 1994).

Forging partnership ties

A program such as MITS is a powerful resource in a community. The challenge for educators is to forge tighter links with faith-based programs such as MITS. Some of these partnerships might be school-based; however, most will be school-linked. One curriculum goal of such a partnership could be to enhance the delivery of school arts programming. For example, the Performance Company might host a series of dance classes at schools. In partnership with school health classes, the Resource Network could provide peer-led workshops, using movement to teach about teen pregnancy and sexually transmitted diseases.[2] School leaders could award participants with community service credit hours and academic internships for their participation in MITS dance classes at neighborhood venues. Or, alternatively, they could contribute resources that support the MITS incentive system of "income" management.[3] A school-based staff member might serve as a liaison to provide dance instructors with background information on students to help them monitor negative behaviors and absenteeism. These outreach activities link educational leaders to the flow of resources and alliances driving youth development, in a coordinated and balanced endeavor—an example of integrated services, with the school orchestrating a nexus of relationships among administrators, teachers, parents, youth-serving agencies, and religious organizations (see, for example, Fertman, 1993; Loda, 1995; Pulliam, 1994).

Programs such as those offered by FSC Urban Ministries are providing outstanding opportunities for supporting and enhancing children's learning. They are "places of hope" (see McLaughlin, Irby, and Langman, 1994) that nurture and engage inner-city youth. The challenge for educators is to tap these religious sanctuaries.

Conclusion

If the social and emotional needs of children are not being addressed by their current support systems, then schools must reach out to the human and social capital available in the community to help expand that support system. Educators can no longer uphold the notion that "real" learning only occurs inside the schoolhouse doors. There are a growing number of religious organizations that are partnering with schools; these offer considerable potential for meaningful learning opportunities for children, which will better enable them to critically examine themselves and their communities.

One of today's most contentious issues is the place of values and beliefs in society. What better way for schools to begin to address our religious diversity than by opening up a dialogue through partnering, in common pursuit of the well-being of children?

Notes

1. From field notes of an interview with Dana Marschalk, executive director of Moving in the Spirit, November 9, 1994, in Atlanta.

2. This MITS prevention effort is conducted after school in the "preconception series" of dances performed by the Apprentice Corporation. The peer-led workshops are held at several community sites and funded by a grant from the March of Dimes.

3. MITS applies a business procedure to the dance experience so that students are provided consistent opportunities to receive positive reinforcement and taught skills in money management. Specifically, students enter into an incentive system that rewards them with daily points for successful participation in program activities. Successful participation includes such behaviors as being punctual and calling in when sick. Bonus points are given for activities such as teaching class, performing at special events, and helping with office clerical duties. At the end of their term, depending upon the incentive system in place at the site, students will have earned enough points or "MITS dollars" for rewards such as a pizza party, gift certificates from a local record store, coupons for grocery store purchases, or transportation vouchers. These rewards are funded by MITS with in-kind expenses from each community site.

References

Brazier, A. M. *Black Self-Determination: The Story of the Woodlawn Organization*. Grand Rapids, Mich.: William B. Eerdmans, 1969.

Caplan, N., Choy, M., and Whitmore, J. *Children of the Boat People: A Study of Educational Success*. Ann Arbor: University of Michigan Press, 1991.

Cordeiro, P., Reagan, T., and Martinez, L. *Multiculturalism and TQE: Addressing Cultural Diversity in Schools*. Thousand Oaks, Calif.: Corwin, 1994.

Drennan, M. "Spiritual Healing." *Education Week*, June 5, 1996, pp. 33–38.

Eck, D. "In the Name of Religions." *Wilson Quarterly*, 1993, *17*(4), 99.

Fertman, C. "Creating Successful Collaborations Between Schools and Community Agencies." *Children Today*, 1993, *22*(2), 32–40.

Fish, J. H. *Black Power/White Control: The Struggle of the Woodlawn Organization in Chicago*. Princeton, N.J.: Princeton University Press, 1973.

Hale-Benson, J. *Black Children: Their Roots, Culture, and Learning Styles*. Baltimore, MD: Johns Hopkins University Press, 1986.

Heath, S. B., and McLaughlin, M. W. "Learning for Anything Everyday." *Journal of Curriculum Studies*, 1994, *26*(5), 471–489.

Hill, S. (ed). *Handbook of Denominations in the U.S.* (9th ed.). Nashville, Tenn.: Abington Press, 1990.

Loda, F. A. "Meeting the Developmental Needs of Adolescents." *Principal*, 1995, *74*(3), 10–11.

Lortie, D. *Schoolteacher*. Chicago: University of Chicago Press, 1975.

Lynch, J., and Hanson, D. *Multicultural Education: Principles and Practices*. London: Routledge and Kegan Paul, 1992.

Maxwell, J. "YFC Celebrates Golden Year." *Christianity Today*, October 3, 1994, *38*(11), 72–73.

McLaughlin, M., Irby, M., and Langman, J. (1994). *Urban Sanctuaries*. San Francisco: Jossey-Bass.

Mincy, R. B. (ed.). *Nurturing Young Black Males: Challenges to Agencies, Programs, and Social Policy*. Washington, D.C.: Urban Institute Press, 1994.

Nowak, J., and Rotunda, R. *Constitutional Law* (4th ed.). St. Paul, Minn.: West Publishing, 1991.

Pulliam, B. "Building Coalitions for Stronger Schools." *Thrust for Educational Leadership*, 1994, *24*(2), 34–35.

Stevens-Arroyo, A. M., and Diaz-Stevens, A. M. "Latino Churches and Schools as Urban Battlegrounds." In S. W. Rothstein (ed.), *Handbook of Schooling in Urban America*. Westport, Conn.: Greenwood Press, 1993.

Tanner, D., and Tanner, L. *The History of Curriculum*. New York: Macmillan, 1990.

Tyack, D. *Turning Points in American History*. Waltham, Mass.: Blasidell, 1967.

RICHARD D. LAKES *is assistant professor of educational policy studies at Georgia State University, Atlanta. He was the editor of* Critical Education for Work *(Ablex, 1994).*

PAULA A. CORDEIRO *is associate professor in the Department of Educational Leadership at the University of Connecticut.*

*The perspectives of educators provide a vehicle for examining
the impact of a two-year partnership between a school, business,
and university. Recommendations for others interested in
forming similar partnerships are provided.*

7

A university, business foundation, and school working together

Betty Merchant

TODAY'S PUBLIC SCHOOL EDUCATORS are being encouraged to involve a broad range of participants in their efforts to improve the educational outcomes of students. Businesses, foundations, and universities have been among the most active participants in attempting to influence the goals, processes, and products of schooling. Businesses and foundations typically provide three kinds of support to schools: money, people, and ideas for reform (Landgren, 1990). They can also play an important role in facilitating partnerships between schools and colleges (Jones and Maloy, 1988). Cross-institutional collaboration can be an extremely complex process, and potential collaborators may hold very different beliefs about the goals and purposes of schooling as well as the means for achieving them.

This chapter describes the efforts of three schools, a university, and a business foundation to establish a multiple constituency model of collaboration for the purposes of improving student achievement. (For the purposes of confidentiality, pseudonyms are

NEW DIRECTIONS FOR SCHOOL LEADERSHIP, NO. 2, WINTER 1996 © JOSSEY-BASS PUBLISHERS

used to refer to the participants.) The perspectives of participating principals, teachers, counselors, and parents provide a vehicle for examining the impact of the collaborative at the local school site and for generating recommendations for others who may be interested in similar partnerships.

Background

In the fall of 1992, the Husk Foundation entered the first phase of its five-year commitment to an educational partnership with the college of education at a midwestern university and three public elementary schools. The purpose of the partnership, the Systemic Design Collaborative, was to develop a replicable model integrating a site-based management approach with best educational practices derived from empirical research and practical experience, to improve student achievement.

Under the general plan implemented by their agreement, university faculty members and Husk Foundation staff composed the collaborative's management group. The Husk Foundation gave Brad Hill, a former school superintendent who had worked extensively with the foundation, responsibility for running the collaborative. He was assisted by foundation facilitators assigned to work directly with principals and teachers in the partner schools. The university's contribution was specified as providing relevant research in the areas of curriculum, pedagogy, and organization; assisting in data collection and analysis; and helping with documentation and evaluation.

Goals for the elementary school design set by the collaborative's management group included high student achievement and parent satisfaction, successful replication in other schools, flexibility and capability for change and growth, and efficient allocation of resources. In addition, the group determined that the design had to encourage the development of an organizational culture in which continual improvement and regular commitment of resources for research and development would be the norm.

Design of the study

At the request of the Husk Foundation in the spring of 1995, I conducted interviews with participants from each of the three schools involved in the collaborative's pilot phase, to obtain their perspectives about the partnership. The goal was to obtain a better understanding of the experiences of participants (principals, teachers, counselors, and parents) in the first two implementation years of the collaborative and to draw from their experiences concerns and recommendations that could be used to improve the effectiveness of the partnership.

In-depth interviews were scheduled with principals in the fall and spring of the 1994–95 school year. Interviews were tape-recorded and transcribed for the purpose of identifying emerging themes. Follow-up telephone interviews were also conducted to clarify information when necessary. In May 1995, interviews were conducted with five members of the building leadership teams (BLTs) and design teams (DTs) from each of the three schools. Individual or focus-group interviews lasting from thirty to forty-five minutes were scheduled.

Administrative themes

Themes voiced by building principals focused on their leadership roles and their relationships with teachers and with Husk Foundation representatives.

Getting acquainted: A matter of time and trust

The principals in the three partnership schools had been assigned to their schools for varying time periods. One had been principal for eleven years, while the other two had been assigned to their buildings for less than two years. Of these two principals, one had the benefit of being phased into her new position during the preceding spring, when she spent one morning a week becoming familiar with the school.

The interviews indicated that the principal who had been in his school the longest had an advantage over his colleagues with respect to his ability to work effectively and efficiently with his staff at moving the work of the collaborative forward. Commenting on his tenure at the school, he stated, "This is my community. I mean, the police bring the kids to me, but that comes after twelve years. I can see it as not working as well as if I had come new when Husk started. If they're looking to move to other schools, I think that they need to choose schools that have had a principal for at least two or three years."

His observation on the benefits of having experience in a school prior to entering the collaborative was supported by the other principals' interviews.

The principal who had been able to become acquainted with her school several months before assuming administrative duties was able to use this experience to help her work with staff members in implementing the collaborative. In the spring prior to moving to the school, she participated in an all-school meeting in which she and the staff discussed a vision for the school and talked about the basic ideas involved in the team.

Before school was dismissed for the summer, the BLT had been formed, as had two DTs. In reflecting on her experiences in the first year of the collaborative, this principal observed that she arrived in the building when the collaborative had already been accepted by teachers: "It wasn't my pet project coming in as a new principal," she said. "Because of that, I think I felt like I was coming on board on an equal level. We were all on a new adventure together."

Her counterpart, on the other hand, who had had little time as an administrator, had greater difficulty in trying to respond to the spirit of the collaborative. Lacking adequate knowledge of her staff, she thought there was a core group committed to Husk but couldn't identify it. As a consequence, this principal stated that she "misjudged staff attitudes" and "blindly chose the building leadership team, without knowing the strengths and weaknesses of the teachers." Her experience underscored the need for building administrators to have sufficient time to become well acquainted with teachers prior to entering a collaborative partnership.

Data from the principals complement the literature on site-based management, which identifies trust as an essential ingredient of such endeavors. All three principals identified the importance of adequate time to become acquainted with staff members' strengths and weaknesses as a top priority. They also saw it as a means of establishing the level of mutual trust that is a prerequisite of successful collaboration. When decision making is shared, traditional responsibilities and relationships change. Mutual trust is required to ensure that all opinions are respected and the collective good of the school is served. Teachers need to trust that they will be provided with the resources necessary to make reasonable input into decision making and that their opinions will be taken seriously by administrators. Administrators need to trust that teachers will approach their new responsibilities with serious purpose and will make decisions in the best interests of all.

Gradually moving from hierarchical to site-based management

Although all three principals described themselves as philosophically committed to shared leadership, their participation in the collaborative afforded them an opportunity to examine more closely how they implemented this concept in their schools. In addition, the principals had to deal with a range of staff members' conceptions of leadership, which either supported or contradicted the idea of advocating site-based management through the collaborative. Trying to represent a clear and consistent model of shared leadership to staff members who were not used to such a model was one of the issues that faced all three principals.

One of the principals described herself as "used to working with teachers in buildings that were collaboratively organized"; but when she arrived at her current school, she found the teachers to be "very traditional and not up-to-date with research." She discovered that the first DT "wanted the principal to be very structured." The principal noted that later, however, she and the teachers tried to find a middle road: "Teachers look to how parents and students should change, not themselves." Although committed to site-based management in principle, she observed, "It's tough to empower—I'm kind of a power person myself, like an island in myself, trying to run school improvement programs. I'm still driving the designs. The scheduling and monitoring are all being done by me, although the design team is coming up with their own ideas." The other principals revealed similar tensions in their interviews.

One principal commented that the conflict between professing a belief in shared leadership and translating it into action was evident. She described the difficulty in trying to "make the shift from being responsible for projects, initiatives, problems and concerns that go on in the building to a site-based decision-making model." She explained it this way:

A lot of the time in prior years, I've been in situations where I've worked on or planned, either by myself or with the help of others, in a way to control them so that the outcome would be positive. Now as we go through this process, I'm not on every design team, and I don't mean that it is necessary, but I find myself wanting to help with the design of everything on the front end to ensure it's a success. I am trying, and gradually moving to, a position of providing necessary input from my position and then sitting back and saying, "If that's what the staff wants, it's fine, and if they don't, it's okay."

Systemic change: Intensive time commitment, gradual progress

All three principals underscored the length of time required by the change effort. One principal commented, "This fall, the district said not to take on another thing but to monitor and revise. We felt we had to overload initially to get things going." She specified that more time was needed to develop the BLT and more assistance was required to help monitor implementations in the classrooms, as not all of the teachers were implementing DT recommendations on a regular basis.

Another principal claimed that the collaborative had underestimated the difficulty of restructuring the individual school. She explained, "You have to have unanimity in the staff to do this, because it requires a lot of time with no extra money. We've had some tough moments here, and there's still some to come. . . . It hasn't been a bed of roses." Gradual progress in bringing about change was a common concern in the principals' reflections on the collaborative's efforts.

Change through increased participation

In addition to their commitment to site-based management and their acknowledgment of the extra time required by this model of leadership, all three principals felt that the increased level of participation by teachers and parents was an important mechanism for addressing the needs of their schools. The work of the principals in participating in the collaborative overlapped many of their other responsibilities, such as responding to state and district mandates for curriculum revision and state quality review processes. All of these efforts added to the administrative workload, but they also benefited the three schools and their students.

One principal discussed the increased work and involvement of parents in the learning process: "The presence of the BLT and the DTs, as well as the parent involvement component, complicates my job and has increased my workload."

Another principal commented on changes in teacher participation in decision making: "This is probably one of the least stressful years I've had, because everybody has ownership in what we choose to do here." He explained that he took decisions to the BLT, but after they had shared responsibility for some decisions, "They told me to do what I think is right, or they said they don't want to make certain kinds of decisions anymore once they've done them a few times."

Benefits of participation

The principals specified five important benefits associated with participation in the collaborative:

- Additional financial resources for instructional materials, program support, substitute teachers, and consultants, allowing the schools to more effectively address student needs
- Training sessions on site-based management and team building
- Guidance and support from facilitators (rated highly by teachers and administrators)
- Technical assistance in grant writing
- Review of educational literature provided by the university to members of the DTs, to update them on relevant research and assist them in identifying best instructional practices

Specific comments from principals offered additional insight into the benefits they associated with participating in the collaborative. Regarding the implementation of improvement plans, one principal said, "The Husk Foundation has been the first to get any concrete improvement plans off the ground at this school." Commenting on the preparation for changes within the school, another principal said, "No one is thrown into things without preparation, in contrast to accelerated schools in the early days . . . and other projects in the district where no one has a clue where to start."

Summing up the overall impact of the collaborative's effort in his school, one principal explained that the collaborative "is everything that I thought it would be and more. . . . I'm convinced that this is the way to do business in a school, and for me personally, it's been an extremely positive opportunity for professional growth."

Administrative concerns and recommendations

The principals identified three major areas of concern related to their participation in the Systemic Design Collaborative: *time* to pursue the work of the collaborative, *compensation* for after-school work, and *continuity* of the collaborative in case of administrative transfers.

These administrators offered eight recommendations based on their two years of participation in the collaborative:

1. *Communicate the goals of the collaborative more clearly to all school personnel.* In one school, teachers thought that the foundation was going to improve the physical facilities.

2. *Use principals who have worked effectively with the Husk Foundation to serve as mentors for new principals coming into the collaborative.* In addition to working as public representatives for their schools, principals in the collaborative can help new administrators understand how partnership schools operate and what their role will entail.

3. *Hold a half-day workshop on social interaction and interpersonal communication skills.* An appropriate interaction topic might be the role of the staff in communicating with the Husk Foundation. The principals felt that having an in-service workshop on interpersonal relationships was not as important for a principal who was well acquainted with his or her staff as it might be for new principals. The workshop could, therefore, be held for new principals as part of their orientation to working in the collaborative.

4. *Work on improving parent involvement.* Although the collaborative has had some impact on this, principals expressed that improvement in this area has been marginal.

5. *Provide an on-site Husk Foundation facilitator who can demonstrate particular instructional approaches and interact personally with teachers.* The sustained presence of a Husk Foundation representative is an incentive for teachers to be accountable for implementing DT recommendations.

6. *Help the schools celebrate their accomplishments more.* Teachers would like district administrators and the Husk Foundation to help them celebrate the achievements of their students. Special recognition through luncheons for teachers, school decorations, charting student progress for public display, and appearances by Husk Foundation officials would boost participant morale.

7. *Direct more leadership and design training toward principals, in addition to working with teachers, and give special attention to the*

principals' changing roles as a result of their involvement in the col-laborative. Principals need more cutting-edge material to keep them moving forward.

8. *Develop a strategy that would allow the collaborative to respond effectively to the departure of a principal from a partner school.* In-service orientation of a new principal should not be left up to the school staff. As one principal pointed out, "The collaborative is still not sufficiently faculty-driven for a new administrator coming in to depend on teachers for assistance."

Leadership team and design team concerns and recommendations

A number of themes emerged from the interviews with BLT and DT members. A majority of these themes reflect the participants' frustrations in trying to respond to the intent of the collaborative.

The bottom line in decision making

The majority of people interviewed expressed a sense of being directed by the Husk Foundation, although not everyone perceived this as negative. One person who serves on both a BLT and a DT said, "I enjoy working with the Husk Foundation. I would not leave that system, necessarily. But I have very much had the sense of being led in certain directions. For example, the research that's been brought to us, although very valid, has been one-sided. It hasn't been, 'Well, should we try this or this or this?' It's been, 'This looks like a real nice way to go' and 'Let's read this and see what it says.'"

A different perspective was presented by a teacher who served on a DT for two years: "I've heard that the Husk Foundation pressured a DT to get things done by the end of the year. My DT was not under that kind of pressure. The Husk Foundation was pretty open as far as what we wanted." Another teacher from the same school said, "I have taken this [Husk Foundation influence] as leading, to make sure we're heading in the right direction instead of just sitting, not knowing where to go from one moment to the next." Although Husk Foundation leadership is accepted by some teachers as necessary for progress, others are inclined to resist what they perceive as pressure to take predetermined pathways in making decisions or to accept decisions that were already made.

The value of time spent

In assessing whether or not the time spent in BLT and DT meetings was worth the energy expended (compared to other ways they might have used their time), participants reported mixed emotions. Some staff members expressed considerable frustration over the additional hours spent on site-based management activities, while other teachers tended to emphasize the rewards of participation. One DT member said, "The time spent on the DT has been worth it for me. If asked again, I would join another DT or BLT." Another DT member agreed, "I feel it has been very worthwhile. I wouldn't have traded it for anything, really." A second-year teacher characterized her participation on a DT as relevant to her own concerns as a new teacher: "Last year, I had a very difficult class, and it was my first year of teaching, so it was really hard for me to give up that time and go to meetings. On the other hand, I can already see the benefits. . . . We're addressing the issues that have bothered me." Although the benefits of their participation in the collaborative are evident to the teachers, they are feeling the stress of responding to the multiple roles demanded in their professional and private lives.

Unfulfilled promises and unexpected contradictions

Interviewees voiced their concern over what they interpreted as unfulfilled promises and contradictions they did not anticipate. Staff members at one school felt that district administrators were confronting their DT with limitations rather than providing the support they had promised. Relatively minor disappointment with the Husk Foundation included the inability of the collaborative to install classroom telephones within the promised time frame and failure of the foundation to deliver book racks to store books acquired by students on their annual foundation-sponsored book-store visit. A more serious disappointment occurred when teachers in one school were encouraged to order supplies and a teacher was told to give her colleagues catalogs from which to place these orders. She reported, "I was told to give catalogs to teachers for them to choose things. They did, and then when I brought the order back, I was told, 'Oh no, not that one.' What am I going to do? I got stuck in the middle of this. It messes up colleagues' relationships sometimes."

Learning the process

In comparing the time spent on learning the processes associated with site-based decision making with the amount of time spent addressing issues of teaching and learning, the majority of team members reported that although their activities had focused largely on process up to this point, teams were now spending more time on matters of instruction. One individual summarized it in this way: "As for addressing the needs of learning, that has been a very time-consuming process, and the time lines for products were unrealistic—hoping for too much, too soon."

For the majority of DTs, the 1995–96 academic year was the first year in which team recommendations were implemented. At the conclusion of this implementation year, it will become more apparent whether the work that has gone into learning the processes associated with change has been worthwhile or if the time and energy have been wasted.

Additional work without compensation

Interviews revealed a great deal of dissatisfaction with the fact that participation in the collaborative involves quite a bit of additional work for teachers, without the benefit of added compensation. As one teacher stated, "One thing people have been upset about is that there is never any reward for all the extra time you have to put in. For example, they want us to get together during the summer, and they'll give us $150 worth of manipulatives [for math students], but it doesn't do anything for us." Although teachers said they were transported to the two-day summer meetings and received accommodations and meals at no cost to them, they were unhappy that no stipend was provided.

One teacher captured the feelings of many of them, saying, "The part I don't like is when I feel we're being treated like employees [of the Husk Foundation]. It's nice to be appreciated, and sometimes I don't get the impression that we are." It appears that many teachers perceive that their extra work is taken for granted and that the additional time and energy put into the collaborative has become an expected part of their regular job.

LT and DT members identified two major areas of concern in discussing their participation in the collaborative: their relationship with the Husk Foundation, and difficulty in correlating student improvements with innovations initiated by the collaborative. They expressed these concerns in the following questions: "Is the Husk Foundation spreading itself too thin by taking on new schools and not increasing its own personnel? What will happen when Husk pulls out? Why do students' scores on standardized tests not show the improvement that teachers believe is occurring?" LT and DT members offered three recommendations to improve the collaborative: keep DTs small (about 5 members), limit the number of goals, and provide stipends for teachers for work completed beyond school hours.

Teachers appreciate something tangible in recognition for what they have accomplished. The grant money some teachers received with a facilitator's assistance was greatly appreciated. District recognition through credit on the salary schedule is another possibility. Recognition through award ceremonies, dinners, or the purchase of teaching supplies would offer incentives, which teachers need to continue their high level of effort.

Conclusion

Questions of concern and recommendations for improvement by the principals and the LT and DT members were generally directed at achieving the goals of the collaborative. The availability of time to do the work and the amount of work to be done were major focuses of all the participants. In addition, the principals and the LT and DT members all expressed concern about the need for compensation for the extra work required by participation in the collaborative. The teachers strongly felt the need for recognition as well as compensation for their work beyond the regular school day, and the principals were very interested in determining how such compensation could be accomplished.

The principals' concern for continuity, given the possibility of changes in administrative assignments, was evidence of their consciousness of the change in their leadership roles as participants in the collaborative. Teachers were also concerned about the future of the partnership, particularly in how changes in financing the collaborative's work would affect the program.

Even with the concerns and reservations expressed by all the participants, the value they placed in the goals of the collaborative and their continued interest in pursing those goals was clear. Forming partnerships across several institutions is extremely complex. Close attention to participants' concerns and the recommendations suggested in this study may lead to improvements in collaborations between schools, businesses, and universities.

References

Jones, B. L., and Maloy, R. W. *Partnerships for Improving Schools.* New York: Greenwood, 1988.

Landgren, C. R. "Educational Partnerships: Sharing the Money, People and Ideas—Review Essay." *Economics of Education Review*, 1990, *9*(2), 181–185.

BETTY M. MERCHANT *is assistant professor at the University of Illinois, Champaign.*

This chapter offers the reader two theoretical frameworks for analyzing the nature of interorganizational collaborative relationships: the public choice and organizational economics.

8

Understanding the organizational dynamics of collaborative partnerships: Two frameworks

Bob L. Johnson, Jr., Patrick F. Galvin

IN AN ATTEMPT TO IMPROVE THE QUALITY of education experienced by students in America's public schools, initiatives designed to link education, social services, and other critical student-support services are being considered and enacted by policymakers across the country. Several larger environmental and political factors appear to have prompted these initiatives. Foremost among these is the task of preparing students for the challenges of the twenty-first century, particularly those considered to be "at risk." In fulfilling this charge, policymakers and practitioners find themselves at a critical juncture. Faced with an ideological shift toward government decentralization, increased demands for services, increased frustrations from constituents over the costs and fragmented nature of current social service delivery systems, and decreasing state revenues, policymakers face the political challenge of reducing costs while at the same time increasing the quality of service delivery and impact. Amidst these and other pressures, and as a means of addressing these demands, interagency collaboration in the delivery of social services has emerged as a viable policy strategy.

NEW DIRECTIONS FOR SCHOOL LEADERSHIP, NO. 2, WINTER 1996 © JOSSEY-BASS PUBLISHERS

As an idea, the move toward school-centered service partnerships appears to be consistent with growing sentiments concerning the importance of local communities in solving pressing social problems (Etzioni, 1993). As noted by Assistant Secretary of Education Sharon Robinson, "the time has come to recapture the spirit of community, the spirit of kinship and neighborliness that is essential to our national well-being . . . to bring together grassroots, community problem-solvers who [will] make it possible for vulnerable children and families to find success" (U.S. Department of Education, Office of Educational Research and Improvement, and the American Educational Research Association,1995, iii, vii).

Indeed, such communitarian sentiments are reflected in two important pieces of legislation recently considered by Congress. The Goals 2000: Educate America Act and the reauthorized version of Title I, the Elementary and Secondary Education Act (ESEA) underscore the importance of local communities' addressing challenging social problems. Both call for localized school-centered service partnerships. Further, this same communitarian spirit is reflected in a number of school-based partnerships that have appeared across the United States.

Although the movement toward coordinated educational and social services is still nascent, the rhetoric surrounding its potential appears to be in full bloom. For many of their most vocal advocates, school-based partnerships provide the means of addressing a wide variety of social challenges. Of interest for researchers and practitioners are questions regarding the workable realities of collaborative initiatives. More specifically, what do we *know* about school-based partnerships, and what do we *need to know* about school-based partnerships? These represent relevant yet challenging questions.

The purpose of this chapter is to offer the reader two theoretical frameworks for conceptualizing the nature of interorganizational collaborative relationships: the public choice and organizational economics. In pursuing this purpose, this chapter offers a macro view of school and interagency collaborative efforts. Its intent is to provide both theorist and practitioner with two sets of lenses for conceptualizing these efforts. Each model is derived from the political science and economics literatures and utilizes the language and logic of politics and economics to frame partnership efforts between organizations. These frameworks have received relatively little attention in the educational literature. This lack of attention is not indicative of their potential contribution to current discussions of educational collaboratives, however.

Political economy, public choice theory, and interagency partnerships

The concept of the political economy has a long and somewhat ambiguous life in the history of the social sciences. The concept has been used to describe, explain, and link a variety of political and economic phenomena in an equally wide variety of settings. Yet, in spite of these difficulties, a review of this literature reveals identifiable strands or clusters of thought in which the concept has been used in a fairly consistent way.

Public choice theory

Among such strands is a body of literature that has emerged in recent years, a variant of political economy known as public choice theory (Buchanan and Tullock, 1962). Using economic reasoning and analysis to explain individual and collective human behavior, public choice theory incorporates several ideas from neoclassical economics. Foremost among these are the ideas of choice, scarcity, exchange, and utility maximization.

Choice, as driven by self-interest, is a fundamental assumption of public choice theory. Human behavior, both individually and collectively, can be understood in terms of the rational pursuit of self-interest within exchange relationships (Becker, 1976). Utility maximizers are individuals who seek to benefit from the exchanges made within a given social system or systems. In articulating this assumption, it should be noted that such a realization does not preclude the possibility that individuals are interested in others and their welfare; it does suggest, however, that most people identify more easily with their own concerns than with those of others. Maximizers following their strongest impulses in a social system act much like economic agents in the economy: they are capable of organizing their objectives in some order of relative importance, and they prefer to get more rather than less out of exchanges.

Closely coupled with the idea of choice is the concept of scarcity. In pursuit of the maximization of self-interest, the individual often encounters conditions of scarcity and accompanying uncertainty. Not only does the object of pursuit often exist in scarce supply, but the resources available to the individual or group for pursuing this object are likewise scarce (for example, time, money, and energy). Few, if any, individuals or groups have the resources to fully maximize all their interests. As a consequence, individuals must choose the best way possible to utilize or allocate in exchange relationships the resources available to them. Whether it is time, money, or energy being allocated, the individual or group must economize in order to realize its most important needs and wants. Understanding and describing the means-ends calculus that defines the economizing process lies at the heart of public choice theory. Whether individually or collectively, human behavior and actions are conceptualized as functions of this calculus.

As a variant of political economy, public choice theory is relatively new. Two additional works are worthy of further note. Each links individual and organizational behavior using the framework and logic of public choice theory.

In an examination of the dynamics of interest-group organization, Olson (1965) seeks to identify those conditions that evoke cooperation among individuals. According to Olson, the benefits of interest-group influences are public and subject to "free riders"—that is, the benefits reaped by the group are enjoyed by individuals and groups who are neither part of the group nor bear the costs of group membership. Further, the costs associated with excluding nonmembers from these benefits are high. As a result, a disincentive exists for individuals to join interest groups. To counteract this state and to ensure the continued and increased participation in the group by individual members, Olson stresses the importance of selective incentives—payments or rewards to participants beyond the free-ride, public-good benefits. Using the logic of public choice, he argues that such incentives are needed to evoke and maintain cooperation from individuals in the group. Hence, the selective incentives offered by the interest group are exchanged for cooperation from individual members, both actual and potential.

A second work in the public choice vein worthy of note is that of William Niskanen (1971). Using the public choice framework, Niskanen attempts to describe and explain the behavior of individual bureaucrats (individuals) and bureaus (collectives or organizations) in the federal and state governments. Like businessmen, bureaucrats and bureaus attempt to maximize their interests. Whereas businessmen battle to maximize profits, bureaucrats and bureaus seek to maximize a different set of variables: salary, perquisites, power, and prestige. This is done by increasing the size of the budget and the bureau. In describing their relationship with other entities and organizations in the environment, Niskanen depicts bureaus as budget-maximizing organizations, capable of expanding far beyond an efficient size and lacking the incentive to trim costs (Niskanen, 1975).

The logic, concepts, and ideas associated with public choice theory can be identified in the organizational theory and education policy literatures, though they are less extensive there than in the fields of political science and economics. In the field of organizational theory, the logic of public choice can be discerned in a set of theories that examine the relationship shared between an organization and its environment. More specifically, *resource-dependence theory* seeks to explain organizational behavior in terms of the following: the flow or exchange of resources between organizations, the dependencies and power differentials created as a result of unequal resource exchange between organizations, the constraining effects dependence has on organizational action, and the efforts by organizational leaders to reduce dependence and maximize autonomy (Pfeffer and Salancik, 1978; Benson, 1975). With its emphasis on resource exchange and autonomy maximization, resource-dependence theory represents a political economy model (this is, a public choice variant of sorts) of organizational and interorganizational behavior (Johnson, 1996).

School-based collaboration policy

Considered together, these efforts in political science and organizational theory suggest that the public choice framework may indeed provide a useful framework for understanding current interagency partnership efforts in education. Further, public choice theory highlights aspects of collaboration that have not been considered by many advocates of educational partnerships. In making this claim, the following observations are offered for consideration.

- *Though mandated by some authoritative legislative body, efforts to form partnerships will ultimately be guided by the efforts of organizational leaders to maximize individual and organizational interests.* The public choice framework suggests that rational, self-interested individuals, acting individually or collectively, will seek to maximize their own welfare within the context of the organizational or institutional reward structures they face. In making this observation, the difficulties surrounding attempts to aggregate individual actions and behavior to the organizational level come to the fore. Public choice theory suggests that organizational leaders will choose to collaborate and interact with those organizations or entities in their environments that have potential to improve the status and position of their organization within its larger environment.

- *The existence of multiple organizations in a single partnership points to the existence of multiple organizational interests and incentive structures.* When considering a single organization, it would appear that two sets of interest or incentive structures at two distinct yet interrelated levels are evident. The first is that of the individual. From the individual's perspective, the organization presents both opportunities to maximize self-interest and restrictions on any attempts to do so. Public choice theory suggests that within a given organization's incentive structure, individuals seek to maximize their own welfare. Given this logic, the following questions regarding collaboration at the individual level appear relevant:

- Does the reward structure of the organization provide incentives for individuals to engage in *intra*organizational partnerships?
- Does the reward structure of the organization provide incentives for individuals to engage in *inter*organizational partnerships?

The existence of multiple interests and incentive structures across collaborating organizations suggests that they may or may not have internal incentive structures conducive to interorganizational collaborative efforts.

The issue is further complicated when one considers a higher level of analysis: the organization. For theorists interested in the nature of interorganizational relationships, this is the primary level of importance. In the context of school-based partnerships, public choice theory highlights the importance of identifying the interests driving the dominant coalitions of each organization in the collaborative. What is it that each organization is seeking to maximize? Are such interests conducive to a functional or dysfunctional collaborative effort?

- *For collaborative efforts to be established and maintained over time, compatible interests and incentive structures must exist between collaborators.* Although collaborative efforts may be mandated, public choice theory suggests that the ultimate success of such efforts does not rest upon the mandate itself but upon the compatibility of interests between individuals and organizations in the partnership. That no two organizations have the same set of incentive structures and vested interests would seem obvious. The concern here, however, is not with the similarity of interests but with their compatibility. In making this distinction, it is worth noting that organizational interests may be similar enough to make collaborative efforts incompatible, or divergent enough to make such efforts complementary.

- *Interagency collaboration policies need to be evaluated in terms of the degree to which the organizational incentives and interests represented*

in a given partnership facilitate or hinder the realization of desired ends.
This caveat highlights the importance of crafting policies that
reflect an awareness of the need for a compatible set of interests
among potential partners. It likewise underscores the possibility
that such compatibility may neither exist nor be possible. From a
public choice perspective, and independent of the communitarian
sentiments driving the policy, this would appear to be critical. Partnership arrangements need to be evaluated in terms of how variations in the structure of incentives affects interorganizational and
intraorganizational behavior. Hence, the challenge for collaborative efforts becomes to identify collaborative frameworks that facilitate the emergence and enactment of programs structured to
achieve desired ends.

Interagency partnerships

A second, yet distinct, set of lenses for conceptualizing the nature
of school-based partnerships is provided by organizational economics theory. Much like public choice theory, this framework is
rooted in the logic of economic thought. Unlike public choice theory, however, organizational economics has as its focus the efficiency of exchanges within and between organizations. Economic
theories of organization tend to view the organization as a means
by which the costs of organizational transactions and governance
can be minimized (see Williamson, 1986; Barney and Ouchi, 1986;
or Galvin and Barott, 1995). Given the human relations values
underlying calls for interagency collaboration, this focus is somewhat unexpected. One is naturally led to ask how organizational
economics can contribute to our understanding of school-based
partnerships.

The answer to this question is found in a fundamental assumption of the framework. At the heart of economic theories of organization is the assumption that people care about the costs of
working together. *Comparative value* is the economic term for this
idea. When individuals have alternative means to organize an
exchange, they will seek a point of equilibrium at which the cost of
such activities is balanced with the benefits derived. One way to

reduce costs and enhance benefits is to change the structure governing exchanges. Thus, in the context of economic theories of organization, efficiency is the fundamental value driving the way individuals structure arrangements by which repeated exchanges are organized.

In the following sections, the issues of information costs and ownership are addressed relative to the willingness of individuals to invest in the infrastructure necessary to sustain interagency partnerships. Ambiguity about ownership and information costs is typically associated with a tendency to underinvest in infrastructure. Hence it is argued below that well-intentioned plans to promote interagency collaboration based on goodwill and service may lead to a diminished service capacity over time.

Organizational economics and information costs

Barney and Ouchi (1986) observe that managerial decisions are simultaneously social and economic in character. According to these authors, failure to recognize this duality leads to the risk of "either implementing programs that [are] not economically viable, or of choosing economically powerful programs that [can] not be implemented" (p. 3). As an idea, interagency collaboration is indeed powerful. Yet from the organizational economics perspective, the important question is whether it is an *economically viable* idea.

Before turning more directly to the question noted above, definitions of the key ideas and concepts associated with the organizational economics framework are offered for clarification. *Organizational economics*, the term used here to refer to the inquiry described more generically above as economic theories of organization, is based on two behavioral assumptions. The first stems from the work of March and Simon (1958). In a theoretically perfect environment, microeconomists assume that decision makers have complete and perfect information. However, in reality there are limits not only to the amount of information decision makers have regarding a given situation but also to their computational capabilities in dealing with that information. Organizational economics differs from neoclassical assumptions of perfect information and competition by accepting what organizational theorists have long used as a starting point: decision makers are limited in their capacity to know or compute alternative solutions to production and distribution problems. In the words of March and Simon (1958), the rationality of decision makers is "bounded."

The second behavioral assumption of organizational economics concerns the opportunistic nature of human behavior and is identified by Williamson (1986) as *opportunism*. Williamson describes such opportunistic behavior as "self-interest with guile," or, in less stark language, "promises one does not intend to keep" (p. 16). As noted in the discussion of the public choice framework above, opportunistic behavior need not be malicious behavior. Who, for example, has not been party to committee work where one's less-than-full commitment to the project required others to pick up the slack?

In combination, these two assumptions help frame the nature of organizational economics. The possibility that one could misrepresent the quality of a product or service helps explain the need for formulating and writing agreements or contracts (either formally or informally). Legal contracts are expensive and constitute a cost-producing transaction. Indeed, the fact that these costs are not attributable to the production process but rather are necessary to protect one from unethical behavior is why they are called transaction costs. Williamson describes transaction costs as points of friction that drag what otherwise appear to be useful and profitable enterprises below some marginal benefit worth pursuing. In common language, people describe such a situation as not being worth the effort.

Another source of transaction costs is the costs associated with the need to monitor exchange agreements. Since human rationality is bounded (March and Simon, 1958), it is impossible to embody all possible contingencies in legal contracts. Indeed, such monitoring would not be needed if information were perfect and complete. Yet because people are tempted to substitute their own interests for those of their colleagues and employers, monitoring is necessary.

Monitoring is a way of controlling for opportunistic behavior. Much like contracts, it too is costly.

Ownership and the market

Most advocates of collaboration and community building suggest that effective communication is an essential component for the creation of interagency programs. Information about how resources will be used, what goals will be pursued, and the time lines for such efforts are all ingredients of what has been described above as an agreement between agencies. Thus, like many collaborative advocates, organizational economists describe communication as an essential component to successful collaboration. Unlike most advocates of collaboration, however, organizational economists focus attention on how the costs associated with such exchanges affect market and organizational behavior.

Akerlof (1986), for example, makes clear the cost of gathering information on how the quality of services or products affects consumer behavior. Economic theory suggests that consumers will want to discount the cost associated with gathering information necessary for decision making. According to Akerlof (1986), where uncertainty about quality exists, consumers are reluctant to pay full market value, because they are unable to distinguish the good services from the bad. This dilemma has important implications for the market. Good service providers will find their services discounted to the same rate as that of inferior providers. These discounts need not be thought of solely in terms of monetary exchange. Discounting one's reputation or the worth of some service can be just as stinging as monetarily undervaluing a service. These points have important implications for those agencies interested in producing quality services. Unless such agencies have an effective and economical means of distinguishing themselves in the marketplace, they will have to accept the discounted prices. For organizational decision makers, the costs associated with gathering the information needed to adequately reduce this uncertainty may be prohibitive. Although their recourse for action is limited, it seems unlikely that most good service providers will accept such devaluation for long. They can either compromise the quality of their work or get out of the business. In either case, the implications are significant. In an environment where market information is incomplete and suspect, the effect of transaction costs is to drive out the good and leave the mediocre.

• *The influence of such costs on the behavior of individuals and the structures governing the activities of organizations is the focus of organizational economics.* Information costs are relevant to interagency collaborations in numerous ways. Social service agencies have long monopolized this sector of the economy. Hence, one may argue that analogies to market response are inappropriate. Two points, however, suggest that the circumstances and activities of social service agencies should be cast more frequently in terms of market responses. First, the reform agendas of virtually all social service agencies—particularly education—describe their clientele as customers. The call is for educators to be more responsive to the needs of their customers. Describing one's clientele as customers invokes a market metaphor. Social service agencies are not likely to change their basic mandate as not-for-profit organizations, but it is likely that they will increasingly act as nonprofits in a market economy. In such an environment, information costs will strongly influence organizational behavior.

The second point is more directly related to the idea of interagency partnering: individuals are not the only customers served by service agencies. Service agencies frequently provide resources to other agencies as intermediate products. In a collaborative project, the outcomes of one agency often become the resources (inputs) of another. For example, the information provided by a welfare agency may be used by a school to address the needs of a particular student.

Thus, in a very real sense, the market analogy is particularly appropriate and important to understanding the behavior of agencies involved in some form of collaboration. The problems of information costs are particularly important for understanding the willingness of agencies to accept intermediate products in a long, linked production process. The quality of intermediate products passed from one agency to another has important implications for the productive capabilities of agencies bound together in a collaborative arrangement.

Another set of issues raised by applying concepts from organizational economics to the analysis of interagency collaboration is that of *ownership*, or *scope of control*. Many advocates of reform describe, in a derisive manner, issues of ownership and control as matters of turf. The image portrayed is that of individuals who are psychologically bound to their empires. Such a portrayal ignores the real issues of ownership and control that do exist, however. Agencies, for example, work on different time lines. Simple matters, such as the time line driving the completion of needed paperwork, become points of contention over the control of operations. Tension arises from the conflict between serving the internal needs of one's own agency versus serving the needs of a collaborative partner. When agencies vertically integrate, issues of control and administration can be vastly simplified. This contrasts sharply with collaborative arrangements that require administrators to invest considerable time and energy influencing processes in other agencies over which they have limited control. The reason such influence is necessary is because the decisions made in one agency affect the opportunities and productive capabilities of workers in another. The danger associated with this situation would appear obvious. As the result of decisions made by a collaborating organization, the reputation of one's own organization is jeopardized.

Acknowledging transaction costs and ownership issues helps clarify why collaborative policies might be difficult to sustain over time. Use of the organizational economics framework highlights the importance of creating collaborative policies that alter the incentive structures of participating organizations. Further, the framework suggests that promoting partnerships among agencies is not primarily a problem of influencing an individual's disposition about cooperation but a matter of properly structuring the contractual and organizational environment in which individuals work.

Conclusion

The purpose of this chapter has been to outline two theoretical frameworks for conceptualizing the nature of interorganizational collaborative relationships. Inasmuch as each examines a different aspect of such relationships, the frameworks are distinct. Yet, given that each is rooted in the literature and logic of economics, both share similar conceptual heritages. While public choice theory has as its focus an examination of the interests that cooperating organizations bring to the collaborative and a weighing of the costs and benefits associated with entering into these relationships, organizational economics highlights the transaction costs associated with such efforts and suggests that certain cooperatives may in fact increase the transaction costs for the parties involved.

In offering these frameworks, we are aware that these are but two among many. A variety of frames can be used to examine and make sense of school-based partnerships, and the motivated reader is encouraged to investigate such possibilities further. A review of the literature suggests that few have used the public choice or organizational economics frameworks to guide discussion and research efforts in the education sector. It is hoped that the description of the frameworks offered here and the critical variables highlighted by each will encourage and broaden current attempts to understand the nature and feasibility of school-based collaborative efforts.

References

Akerlof, G. A. "The Market for 'Lemons': Quality, Uncertainty and the Market Mechanism." In J. B. Barney and W. G. Ouchi (eds.), *Organizational Economics: Toward a New Paradigm for Understanding and Studying Organizations.* San Francisco: Jossey-Bass, 1986.

Barney, J. B., and Ouchi, W. G. (eds.). *Organizational Economics: Toward a New Paradigm for Understanding and Studying Organizations.* San Francisco: Jossey-Bass, 1986.

Becker, G. *The Economic Approach to Human Behavior.* Chicago: University of Chicago Press, 1976.

Benson, K. J. "The Interlocking Network as a Political Economy." *Administrative Science Quarterly,* 1975, 20, 229–249.

Buchanan, J., and Tullock, G. *The Calculus of Consent.* Ann Arbor: University of Michigan Press, 1962.

Etzioni, A. *The Spirit of Community: Rights, Responsibilities, and the Communitarian Agenda*. New York: Crown Publishers, 1993.

Galvin, P., and Barott, J. "A National Data Base for Organizations: A Proposal for Including Data from Economic Theories of Organization." In R. Ogawa (ed.), *Advances in Research and Theories of School Management and Educational Policy*, Vol. 3.Greenwich, Conn.: JAI Press, 1995.

Johnson, B. L., Jr. "Resource Dependence Theory: A Political Economy Model of Organizations." In J. Shafriz (ed.), *International Encyclopedia of Public Policy and Administration*. New York: Henry Holt, 1996.

March, J. G., and Simon, H. A. *Organizations*. New York: Wiley, 1958.

Niskanen, W. A. *Bureaucracy and Representative Government*. Chicago: Aldine-Atherton, 1971.

Niskanen, W. A. "Bureaucrats and Politicians." *Journal of Law and Economics*, 1975, *18*, 617–643.

Olson, M. *The Logic of Collective Action*. Cambridge, Mass.: Harvard University Press, 1965.

Pfeffer, J., and Salancik, G. R. *The External Control of Organizations: A Resource Dependence Perspective*. New York: Free Press, 1978.

U.S. Department of Education, Office of Educational Research and Improvement, and the American Educational Research Association. *School-Linked Comprehensive Services for Children*. Washington, D.C.: U.S. Government Printing Office, 1995.

Williamson, O. E. *Economic Organization: Firms, Markets and Policy Control*. New York: SUNY Press, 1986.

BOB L. JOHNSON, JR. *is assistant professor of educational administration at the University of Utah. His teaching and research interests are in the areas of education politics, policy development, and schools as organizations.*

PATRICK F. GALVIN *is associate professor of educational administration at the University of Utah. His teaching and research interests include educational finance and organizational economics.*

This chapter reviews the common themes about educational partnerships discussed in previous chapters and provides recommendations for educational leadership preparation programs.

9

The implications of partnerships for the preparation and professional growth of educational leaders

Paula A. Cordeiro, Karen S. Loup

THIS SOURCEBOOK BEGAN by describing a variety of partnerships involving schools and other organizations, including institutions of higher education, families, school-based health centers, nonprofit agencies, religious organizations, and businesses. Additionally, the preceding chapters have presented frameworks for analyzing both educational partnerships and the conditions required for their development and support. The authors used various metaphors to describe the roles of educators who created, developed, planned, nurtured, maintained, and sustained partnerships with schools and their communities, calling them founders, liaisons, negotiators, boundary spanners, and collaborators.

This chapter begins by highlighting common themes that permeate the earlier chapters. Next, rather than describing the leadership roles of school principals or other educational administrators, it examines the multiple conceptions of leadership of the myriad people involved in developing educational partnerships. The chapter explores this central question: if partnering with the community

NEW DIRECTIONS FOR SCHOOL LEADERSHIP, NO. 2, WINTER 1996 © JOSSEY-BASS PUBLISHERS

is crucial for improving student learning, then what implications do these partnership efforts have for practicing educators as well as those preparing for leadership positions? As we observe preparation programs nationwide, some of these changes are already occurring. Given our changing society, the onus is on institutions of higher education and on local, state, regional, and national education organizations to hold preparation programs to the task of preparing leaders who can effectively and creatively address the most vexing problems facing our schools.

Leaders appear as they are needed

Before discussing the skills and knowledge necessary for educational leaders to foster the kinds of partnerships described in this text, it seems necessary to remember that leadership is a behavior that can emerge from anywhere. Merely understanding the issues described here and possessing certain skills will not lead our institutions to create partnerships that will enhance our children's learning. In partnership activities, leadership may be displayed by a teacher, student, central office administrator, project director of a local organization, or parent. How do such behaviors emerge? First, one must be willing to be a leader. In healthy systems leaders appear as they are needed. They serve as leaders by accomplishing what needs to be done. They might continue in this role indefinitely, or they may decide at a later point to withdraw and permit others to lead.

Borrowing a definition from physics, Wheatley (1995) refers to power as "the rate at which work gets done." This definition is significantly different from thinking of power in terms of position. It is evident from some of the chapters in this text that older notions of leadership, which center on position, are quite narrow, especially when one is considering the complexities of educational partnerships.

For example, it is the classroom teachers in Brouillette's study (Chapter Five) who are closest to the writers who visit their classrooms, not the principals. Each teacher personally knows the writer-in-residence and has attended an eleven-week writing seminar with him or her. It is highly unlikely that this collaboration would continue without teacher leadership, because it is through teacher learning and improved student learning that these partnerships have succeeded.

Knowledge and skills needed for educational leaders: Connecting systems

Partnerships can be particularly efficient and beneficial to children when they are connected to the larger system. Whether we analyze a partnership through a public choice or organizational economics framework (Chapter Eight), it is evident that the interests of all involved as well as the transaction costs associated with the partnership must be considered. Identifying who is part of the system may be one of the most challenging questions to answer. For example, parents and families are less often seen as part of the system. As Seitsinger discusses (Chapter Two), the traditional concept of parent involvement in education (for example, attending school open houses) has limited the involvement of family members in a child's growth and development. Expanding the definition of parent involvement to *family* involvement (including the participation of adults unrelated by blood who take part in raising a child) is a necessary first step. Analyzing the multiple roles family members can play is another crucial step for educational leaders. Recognizing the many people who may play a major role in a child's upbringing is crucial to forming a true school-family partnership.

An understanding of theoretical concepts and frameworks is important for educational leaders. For example, if a person is not aware of the public choice and organizational economics frameworks that might be used in analyzing a partnership, then there is a far greater likelihood that key questions will not be broached. In the case of family involvement, if an educator is not aware of the typologies of family involvement developed by researchers such as

Epstein, Ziegler, or Comer (see Chapter Two), then more effective techniques of parent involvement might be overlooked. Such concepts and frameworks are only attempts at explanations; however, a well-prepared educator is familiar with the frameworks and underlying concepts and relationships relevant to the diverse systems involved in educating a child.

Figure 9.1 depicts the many organizations and agencies from the larger system that are possible collaborators in forming partnerships with schools. Tapping the potential of these organizations by forming educational partnerships will expand the assets in a school's community, thus helping to support and educate children.

So, one might ask, what is that knowledge base needed by educational leaders to form partnerships with organizations such as those depicted in Figure 9.1? This knowledge base and the teacher preparation programs that provide it is explored in the following section.

Leadership preparation programs

In the last ten years there has been a clarion call to revamp the preparation of educational leaders (Murphy, 1993; Milstein, 1993). The recommendations presented here are the result of analyzing the current literature in educational leadership (covering a broad base of disciplines, including sociology, economics, psychology, anthropology) in light of the implications of the analyses in this sourcebook.

In an article describing the leadership needed in professional development schools, Teitel (1996) argued that educational leadership preparation programs must review their content in light of what he called "a second level of review . . . to look not only at what we preach but what we practice." He asked, "How many of our programs model the collaborative leadership we espouse to our graduates?" (p. 15).

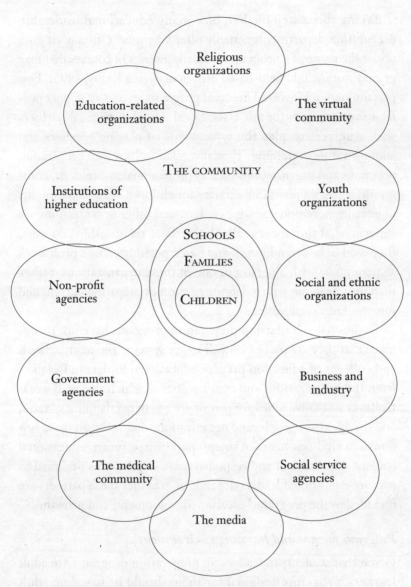

Figure 9.1. Potential Assets for Forming Educational Partnerships.

Taking this a step further, how many educational leadership preparation departments actually offer *programs*? Often what goes under the name of a program is actually a series of courses that may or may not include field-based experiences (see Kraus, 1996). Few practitioners are involved in actual programs, except as adjunct professors or as guests for one class. Local school districts, if partners with a university, play the typical role of placing teachers and administrators in training. Typically, relationships with preparation programs and organizations such as professional associations, community agencies providing services for children, state departments of education, regional service centers, and other organizations are superficial, if they exist at all. When these relationships do exist, they tend to be serendipitous and based possibly on one professor's acquaintance with a person in one of these organizations, rather than on a program with a definite mission of preparing current and future educational leaders.

Traditionally, leadership preparation programs have not recognized that they are part of a much larger system. Too many schools and colleges of education prepare educational leaders in isolation from the organizations and communities in which they will work. Colleges and universities are part of dozens of overlapping systems, and the agencies, people, and organizations that make up these systems are vital resources in the preparation of future educational leaders. The survival and responsiveness of programs designed to prepare educational leaders depends on whether these partners are included in the programs' creation, development, and growth.

Program format and learning environment

Given that students in leadership preparation programs are adult learners, programs designed for them should be based on adult learning principles. Key factors related to learner characteristics that play a role in program format include motivation, feedback, learning style, self-directed learning, age, growth needs, achievement style, locus of control, self-efficacy, goal directedness, and resource availability (see Cordeiro, Kehrhahn, and Sheckley, 1995).

Since the goal of university preparation programs is to transfer learning to the school setting, then the characteristics of the learning environments afforded to students and the instructional design and delivery of elements of programs are crucial.

The learning environment for educational leaders must be supportive and challenging. In an ideal learning setting, support might emanate from several directions, including the field supervisor or mentor, university instructor, and fellow students who are part of the work group. Additionally, programs need to provide task and climate support. Task support includes providing sufficient resources and time; climate support includes providing an environment in which feedback and criticism are encouraged and where safety nets for mistakes are provided.

Graduate programs that meet these adult learning, task, and climate-support needs afford students multiple formats for learning. These formats might include class cohorts or research teams, independent study with regular feedback, group and individual advising, seminars, and multiple apprenticeship opportunities. A growing body of research supports the cohort program format (Roberts, 1993; Barnett and Caffarella, 1992). Thus, providing multiple opportunities and formats to accommodate the unique characteristics of adult learners seems necessary if educational leadership preparation programs are to prepare leaders to deal effectively with teaching in today's complex school environments.

Instructional delivery, design, and techniques

Considering the characteristics of adult learners, a variety of delivery systems should be employed in leadership preparation programs. Rather than providing a series of courses, preparation programs should be designed so that learning activities are connected. In some cases they may be sequenced with planned overlaps in content, rather than falling prey to the enormous amount of overlap that randomly occurs in many preparation programs. Content should be current and relevant, with appropriate theory presented to help explain and interpret relationships in the area of interest.

Programs designed in such ways would afford students multiple opportunities for acquiring declarative, procedural, and context-dependent knowledge (see Cordeiro and Campbell, 1996). These opportunities are enhanced through the various instructional formats that should be a part of all preparation programs.

For example, Ertmer and Cennamo (1995) believe instructional features should include situated learning, modeling, coaching, reflection, articulation, and exploration. Adapting their framework, Kraus (1996) added the additional feature of assessment. These authors contend that effective instruction for enhancing learning includes a cognitive apprenticeship component for each of these instructional features. Features of such cognitive apprenticeships might include learning in multiple contexts, explicit modeling of metacognitive processes, scaffolding of cognitive supports, measurement of cognitive growth, and using diverse problem-solving approaches. Leithwood, Begley, and Cousins (1994) reviewed the research of pre-service and in-service education programs and "generated a significant number of promising instructional techniques" (p. 180). The research literature describes a variety of techniques associated with learning transfer. These techniques include oral and written articulation of educational beliefs, case analyses, goal setting, guided group study, simulations, independent reading and reflection, student-centered lecture and discussion, recognition and reward, and simulated and actual problem-based learning projects, to name but a few. It should be noted that students need to play an active role in all instructional techniques and that some techniques are more appropriate with declarative, procedural, or context-dependent knowledge.

Program content

So much has been written about individual leadership preparation programs that summarizing their core elements and content can be overwhelming (see Murphy, 1993; National Policy Board for Educational Administration [NPBEA], 1989; National Association of Secondary School Principals [NASSP], 1985). The coalescing of forces described in Chapter One that has made long-term collaboration between schools and their external communities necessary is having the same impact on university preparation programs for teachers and administrators. As preparation programs respond to these forces, several overarching themes related to program content can be identified. The language used to describe these themes varies considerably from program to program; however, an analysis of the literature reveals many content similarities. These themes include understandings of self, others, the environment, the shaping of organizations, and the importance of using inquiry.

As preparation programs explore more effective and efficient ways to prepare their students, perhaps more attention might be directed to several areas that have received minimal attention. These areas—organizational communication and interpersonal relations—though linked, are described separately here.

Much of the early literature on communication stressed communicating horizontally and vertically within the organizational hierarchy. This metaphor is no longer appropriate, given the changing contexts of schools and communities. The focus and goal of organizational communication must be to connect the many disparate networks that are part of the larger system. As organizational environments become more interconnected, they become more complex. Thus, facilitating the formation of participation networks will be a major challenge for educational administrators of the future. Colleagueship will need to be redefined. Leadership preparation students will need to better understand their community and the multiple ways of communicating with clients. Technology such as the Internet holds considerable potential for improving the flow of information, but it is only one source for enhancing communication and expanding participation networks. For example, schools with fax machines and classrooms with telephones have the means, through simple mechanisms, to enhance communication opportunities.

Related to improving communication is the issue of language. At the time of this writing, no preparation program literature describes the offering of conversation classes in another language. Demographic projections alone should highlight the importance of educational leaders' understanding the myriad issues concerning language acquisition that are crucial to schools. Additionally, conversational fluency in another language (preferably Spanish because of demographic projections) should be encouraged and supported, as it enhances development of linkages.

The topic of interpersonal relationships has received minimal attention in university preparation programs. A training program such as Interpersonal Process Recall (Kagan and Kagan, 1991) is worthy of the attention of leadership preparation faculty. Additionally, group facilitation, team building, and an understanding of "cultural competence" are vital for future educational leaders. Using instructional approaches as problem-based learning will afford students opportunities to develop and hone group processing skills throughout their preparation.

Program involvement: Connecting to the larger systems

Preparation programs are part of a much larger system, yet too many leadership preparation departments develop and implement programs with minimal involvement from the larger system.

A key question that is rarely asked in the assessment of leadership preparation programs is, "Who is in the system?" The question may not be asked because individuals do not recognize that they or others are part of the same system. As various parts of preparation programs are developed and improved, participation in program components should be extended to groups and individuals who are part of the greater system. These groups might include local school districts; community, state, and national agencies involved with the growth and development of children; professional organizations; and political leaders, to name but a few.

Involving people from the larger system also means vastly expanding communication networks. Technology can play a major role for professors of educational leadership in communicating with other members of the system. Making these external connections may also lead to new opportunities for leadership to emerge from people outside schools and colleges of education in the development of preparation programs. Organizational hierarchies will be flattened, and instead, a series of networks allowing leadership to emerge from all participants will take the lead in preparing future educational leaders. Thus, establishing and maintaining communication networks are not only key to developing partnerships for schools and other organizations, they are also crucial to the development of educational preparation programs themselves.

Conclusion

The concepts and real-life examples detailed in this sourcebook describe various types of educational partnerships and ways to assess their potential contribution to the education of our children. Shrinking school budgets, increasing racial polarization, scarce economic resources, and increased demands for accountability are clarion calls requiring educational leaders to rethink how to accomplish their objectives. Educational partnerships hold considerable potential for addressing these challenges.

References

Barnett, B., and Caffarella, R. "The Use of Cohorts: A Powerful Way for Addressing Issues of Diversity in Preparation Programs." Paper presented at the annual convention of the University Council for Educational Administration, Minneapolis, Minnesota, October 30 to November 1, 1992.

Cordeiro, P., and Campbell, B. "Increasing the Transfer of Learning Through Problem-Based Learning in Educational Administration." Paper presented at the annual convention of the American Education Research Association, New York City, April 8 to 12, 1996.

Cordeiro, P., Kehrhahn, M.,and Sheckley, B. "Effectiveness and Efficiency in Graduate Education: A Case Analysis." Paper presented at the annual conference of the International Forum for Quality in Higher Education, Daytona Beach, Florida, February 1995.

Ertmer, P., and Cennamo, K. "Teaching Instructional Design: An Apprenticeship Model." *Performance Improvement Quarterly*, 1995, *8*(4), 43–58.

Kagan, N., and Kagan, H. "Interpersonal Process Recall." In P. Dorwik (ed.), *Using Video in the Behavioral Sciences*. New York: Wiley, 1991.

Kraus, C. "Administrator Preparation Programs: Impact on Job Preparedness and Learning." Unpublished doctoral dissertation, Department of Educational Leadership, University of Connecticut, 1996.

Leithwood, K., Begley, P., and Cousins, J. B. *Developing Expert Leadership for Future Schools*. Washington, D.C.: Falmer Press, 1994.

Milstein, M. *Changing the Way We Prepare Educational Leaders.* Thousand Oaks, Calif.: Corwin, 1993.

Murphy, J. (ed.) *Preparing Tomorrow's School Leaders: Alternative Designs.* University Park, Penn.: University Council for Educational Administration (UCEA), 1993.

National Association of Secondary School Principals (NASSP). *Performance-Based Preparation of Principals: A Framework for Improvement.* Reston, Va.: Author, 1985.

National Policy Board for Educational Administration (NPBEA). *Improving the Preparation of School Administrators.* Charlottesville, Va.: Author, 1989.

Roberts, J. "Concerns and Development of Cohort Administrators: Foci and Stages." Paper presented at the annual meeting of the American Educational Research Association, Atlanta, Georgia, April 1993.

Teitel, L. "Leadership in Professional Development Schools: Lessons for the Preparation of Administrators." *UCEA Review,* 37(1), 1996, pp. 10, 11, 15.

Wheatley, M. *Applying the New Sciences to School Improvement.* Interview by Dennis Sparks. Audiocassette. Oxford, Ohio: National Staff Development Council 1995.

PAULA A. CORDEIRO *is associate professor at the University of Connecticut and a former principal of the American School of Las Palmas, Spain.*

KAREN S. LOUP *is assistant professor in the department of educational leadership at the University of Georgia. Her research interests include the study of learning environments, self and organizational efficacies, and change and reform in schools.*

Index

Achievement, and values and beliefs,
75–76
Administrators. *See* Principals
Akerlof, G. A., 109, 112
Alternative Learning Centers, 78
American Educational Research Association, 100, 113
Apprentice Corporation, 79–80, 82
Asset mapping, 11
Atlanta, religious organizations in,
79–81
Autonomy, in partnerships, 4

Baltimore, religious organizations in,
77–78
Barnett, B., 121, 125
Barney, J. B., 106, 107, 112
Barott, J., 106, 113
Becker, G., 101, 112
Begley, P., 122, 125
Bempechat, J., 24–25, 28
Benson, K. J., 103, 112
Berla, N., 17, 20, 28
Birth-to-Three, 8
Boehm, M., 26, 28
Boundary spanning: for family involvement, 25–26; with health and human services professionals, 44, 48–50, 51–52; in partnerships, 4, 13
Brazier, A. M., 77, 82
Brouillette, L., 57, 70, 116
Buchanan, J., 101, 112
Buddhism, 74, 76
Building leadership teams (BLTs), and systemic design, 87–88, 90–91, 94–97
Bureaucracies, and public choice theory, 103
Business foundation: and administrative

themes, 87–91; aspects of partnership with, 85–98; background on, 85–86; and benefits of participation, 91–92; conclusion on, 97–98; and disappointments, 95–96; and recommendations, 92–97; study design for, 87

Caffarella, R., 121, 125
Calvinism, 72
Cambridge, Massachusetts, health care in schools of, 42
Campbell, B., 122, 125
Caplan, N., 76, 82
Career High School, and higher education institutions, 33
Catholic Youth Organization, 76
Catholicism, 72, 76
Cennamo, K., 122, 125
Change, systemic, 90–91
Chavkin, N. F., 24, 25, 28
Cheng, N., 13, 14
Chicago, religious organizations in,
76–77, 78
Child Opportunity Zones, 22, 23
China, compradors in, 13
Choice, and maximizers, 101–102
Chou, V., 52, 55
Choy, M., 76, 82
Church of England, 72
Cincinnati, religious organizations in,
78
Clark, B. R., 46, 54
Cleveland, religious organizations in, 78
Cognitive apprenticeships, for leaders,
122
Collaboration. *See* Partnerships
Comer, J. P., 18, 28, 118
Communication: and business foundation, 93; for family involvement,

20; and leadership preparation,
123–124; and organizational
dynamics, 109; in partnerships, 10
Communities: caring, and family
involvement, 24; knowledge of, in
partnerships, 11; and organizational dynamics, 100; professional,
32–34; and religious organizations,
76–77
Community colleges, in partnerships,
35
Comparative value theory, 106–107
Compensation, for partnership partici-
pation, 92, 96–97
Complexity, detailed and dynamic, 6
Comprador concept, 13
Concord, Massachusetts, health care in
schools of, 41
Confucianism, 76
Connecticut, University of, and Profes-
sional Development Center, 33
Contracts, and transaction costs,
108–109
Coontz, S., 19, 28
Cordeiro, P. A., 1, 14, 19, 28, 71, 76,
82, 83, 115, 120, 122, 125, 126
Cortese, P. A., 41, 54
Costs: information, 107–111; transac-
tion, 108–109
Court cases, and religious organiza-
tions, 72–73
Cousins, J. B., 122, 125
Crowson, R. L., 52, 55
Cubais, D., 16, 23
Cultures: and health and human ser-
vices professionals, 45; of higher
education institutions, 36–37; and
organizational dynamics, 111; in
partnerships, 4, 13; of writers and
teachers, 60, 63
Cummings, T. G., 42, 54

Dallas, religious organizations in, 78
Darling-Hammond, L., 32, 39
Decision making, and business founda-
tion, 94–95
Denver, family involvement in, 21, 22
Design teams (DTs), and systemic
design, 87–98
Dewey, J., 54
DeWitt Wallace-*Reader's Digest* fund,
32

Diaz-Stevens, A. M., 76, 83
Dinkins, S., III, 66–69
Drennan, M., 77, 78, 82
Dropouts, programs for, 7–8
Dryfoos, J. G., 42, 54

Eck, D., 74, 82
Economics: organizational, 106–109,
117; political, 101–107
Education of All Handicapped Children
Act of 1975, 18
Elementary and Secondary Education
Act, 100
Environment: defined, 54; for leader-
ship preparation, 120–121; turbu-
lent, 47
Epstein, J. L., 19, 20–21, 28, 118
Ertmer, P., 122, 125
Etzioni, A., 100, 113

Family involvement: advocacy mode of,
18; aspects of, 15–29; background
on, 15–16; bake sale mode of,
17–18; benefits of, 17, 18–19; and
caring communities, 24; conclusion on, 27–28; diversity in, 19;
founders for, 26–27; history of,
17–20; and individuals, 23–24;
and leadership preparation,
117–118; levels of, 20–21; and
principals, 24–27; programs for,
21–22
Family Resource Schools, 21, 22
Family Services Consultation (FSC)
Urban Ministries, 79, 81
Fertman, C., 81, 82
Fiene, R., 18, 28
Finch, F. E., 48, 52, 54
First Amendment, 73
Fish, J. H., 77, 82
Flexibility, for partnerships, 11
Fordham University, and social work
center, 32
Foster, W., 51–52, 54
Foundation. *See* Business foundation
Founders metaphor, 26–27
Fundamentalism, 73

Gage, R., 58, 70
Galvin, P. F., 99, 106, 113
Garden of Prayer Baptist Church,
77–78

Gary, Indiana, religious organizations in, 78
Goals 2000: Educate America Act, 100
Goldring, E. B., 17, 26, 28, 48, 52, 54
Goodlad, J., 37, 39
Greene, A. L., 19, 29

Hale-Benson, J., 75, 82
Hamilton Elementary School, and family involvement, 22
Hanson, D., 75, 83
Hartford, Connecticut, Professional Development Center in, 33
Head Start, 8, 18, 77
Health and human services professionals: aspects of partnerships with, 41–55; boundary spanning with, 44, 48–50, 51–52; conclusion on, 53–54; history of, 41–42; and leadership, 50–53; societal imperative for, 46–48; study of, 43–45; trends for, 42–43
Heath, S. B., 80, 83
Henderson, A., 17, 18–19, 20, 28
Henry, T., 58, 70
Higher education institutions: aspects of partnership with, 31–40; and business foundation, 85–98; conclusion on, 39; problems and possibilities for, 36–39; professional segments of, 33, 35; traditions and trends in, 32–36; urban, 35; vision for, 38
Hill, B., 86
Hill, P., 58, 70
Hill, S., 74, 83
Hinduism, 74
Hoffman, M., 64
Holmes Group, 33, 39
Hooper-Briar, L., 34, 38, 40, 42, 55
Houston Independent School District, writers in, 59–69
Husk Foundation, in partnership with university and schools, 86–88, 92–95, 97

Incentive structures, and organizational dynamics, 104–106
Information costs: and markets, 109–111; and organizational economics, 107–109
Institutions. See Higher education institutions

Interactions, in partnerships, 6–8
Interdependence, with health and human services professionals, 47–48, 52
Interest groups, and public choice theory, 102–103
Interpersonal Process Recall, 124
Involvement. See Family involvement
Irby, M., 81, 83
Islam, 74

Jehl, J., 41, 55
Johnson, B. L., Jr., 99, 104, 113
Jones, B. L., 31, 39, 85, 98
Judaism, 74

Kagan, H., 124, 125
Kagan, N., 124, 125
Kagan, S. L., 21, 28, 42, 55
Kehrhahn, R., 120, 125
Kimbrough, J., 58, 70
Kirby, D., 41, 55
Kirst, M. W., 41, 55, 58, 70
Klein, J., 37, 39
Klugman, E., 42, 55
Knapp, M. S., 36, 40, 52, 55
Knowledge: of community, 11; integrated with writing, 66–69; for leadership preparation, 117–118
Kosciuszyk Middle School, and family involvement, 16
Kraus, C., 120, 122, 125
Kretzmann, J. P., 11, 14

Lakes, R. D., 71, 83
Land grant institutions, in partnerships, 34–35
Landgren, C. R., 85, 98
Langman, J., 81, 83
Lareau, A., 20, 28
Last Poets, 69
Lawson, H. A., 34, 38, 40, 42, 55
Leaders: as compradors, 13; emergent, 5–6, 116–117; in health and human services, 50–53; for partnerships, 5–6, 8–9
Leadership preparation: aspects of, 115–126; conclusion on, 125; delivery systems in, 121–122; format and environment for, 120–121; knowledge and skills needed in, 117–118; and larger systems,

124–125; program content in, 122–124; programs in, 118, 120–125
Leithwood, K., 122, 125
Lerner, R., 3, 14
Levin, R. A., 52, 55
Lipnack, J., 3, 4, 6, 14
Literacy in Motion, 79
Loda, F. A., 81, 83
Lortie, D., 72, 83
Loup, K. S., 115, 126
Lovick, S., 41, 55
Lynch, J., 75, 83

Maçao, compradors in, 13
Maeroff, G., 39, 40
Magic eye art, 6–7
Maloy, R. W., 31, 39, 85, 98
Mann, H., 41
March, J. G., 107, 108, 113
March of Dimes, 82
Markets, and organizational dynamics, 109–111
Marschalk, D., 79, 82
Martin, J., 26, 28
Martinez, L. P., 19, 28, 76, 82
Maxwell, J., 76, 83
McDill, E., 19, 29
McKnight, J. L., 11, 14
McLaughlin, M. W., 32, 39, 80, 81, 83
Meier, D., 15–16, 23, 28
Melnick, S., 18, 28
Merchant, B. M., 85, 98
Michael, D. N., 48, 52, 55
Michigan, charter school in, 32
Milstein, M., 118, 126
Milwaukee, family involvement in, 16
Mincy, R. B., 75, 83
Model Cities, 77
Monroe Kolek, M., 1, 14
Morris, R. D., 19, 29
Moving in the Spirit (MITS), 79–81, 82
Murphy, J., 51, 55, 58, 70, 118, 122, 126

Nardine, F. E., 19, 29
National Association of Retarded Citizens, 18
National Association of Secondary School Principals, 122, 126
National Center for Education Statistics, 58, 70

National Center for Social Work and Education Collaboration, 32
National Education Goals Panel, 17, 29
National Parent-Teacher Association, 17, 29
National Policy Board for Educational Administration, 122, 126
Natriello, G., 19, 29
Neidell, S., 42–43, 55
Neville, P. R., 21, 28
New Beginnings, 21, 22
New Haven, Connecticut, partnerships in, 33
Niskanen, W. A., 103, 113
Noddings, N., 16, 24, 29
Nonprofit organization, writers sponsored by, 57–70
Nowak, J., 73, 83

Office of Educational Research and Improvement, 100, 113
Oklahoma City, religions in, 74
Olson, M., 102–103, 113
One Church/One School, 78
Opportunism, and organizational economics, 108
Organizational dynamics: aspects of, 99–113; background on, 99–101; conclusion on, 112; ownership and markets in, 109–111; and political economy, 101–107
Organizational economics: and information costs, 107–109; and partnerships, 106–107, 117
Ouchi, W. G., 106, 107, 112
Outtz, J. H., 3, 14, 19, 29
Ownership, and organizational dynamics, 109–111

Pallas, A. M., 19, 29
Parents. See Family involvement
Participation benefits, 91–92
Partnerships: aspects of, 1–14; with business foundation, 85–98; changing role of, 2–3; common purpose in, 3–4, 10; conclusion on, 14; factors in successful, 8–12; with families, 15–29; framework for, 3–8; with health and human services professionals, 41–55; with higher education institutions, 31–40; insti-

tutionalizing, 12; and leadership preparation, 115–126; organizational dynamics of, 99–113; and organizational economics, 106–107, 117; potential, 80–81, 119; preconditions for, 8–10; and public choice theory, 101–104, 117; purposes of, 1–2, 71; with religious organizations, 71–83; support for, 10–11; as voluntary, 5; with writers, 57–70

Pennsylvania, University of, in partnerships, 35

Performance Company, 80, 81

Pfeffer, J., 103, 113

Political economy, and organizational dynamics, 101–107

Portner, J., 42, 55

Power, concepts of, 116

Principals: and family involvement, 24–27; and health and human services professionals, 47, 48–53; and systemic design, 87–94

Professional Development Center, 33. See also Leadership preparation

Progressive era, and children's health issues, 41–42

Project Succeed Academy, 78

Public choice theory: and partnerships, 101–104, 117; and schools, 104–106

Pulliam, B., 81, 83

Rallis, S. F., 17, 26, 28, 48, 52, 54

Readiness, for partnerships, 9–10

Reading Recovery, 8

Reagan, T., 19, 28, 76, 82

Reciprocity, in partnerships, 10

Redding, S., 18, 29

Religious organizations: aspects of partnerships with, 71–83; and communities, 76–77; conclusion on, 81–82; diversity of, 74–75; history of, 72–74; potential ties with, 80–81; programs of, 76–80; and separation of church and state, 71–72

Resource-dependence theory, 103–104

Resource Network, 80, 81

Resources, in partnerships, 10–11

Restine, L. N., 31, 40

Rhode Island: Child Opportunity Zones in, 22, 23; departments in, 23

Rice University, writing seminar at, 64

Riis, J., 42

Roberts, J., 121, 126

Robinson, S., 100

Rotunda, R., 73, 83

Saga metaphor, 46

Salancik, G. R., 103, 113

San Diego, family involvement in, 21, 22

Scarcity, and maximizers, 102

Schmidt, B. C., 57, 70

School-based health centers (SBHCs), professionals for, 42–43, 46–51, 54

Schools: criticism of, 57–58; customers of, 110; and public choice theory, 104–106. See also Partnerships

Scopes v. Tennessee, 72–73

Seamlessness, in partnerships, 11–12

Seitsinger, R. M., Jr., 15, 29, 117

Senge, P., 6, 14

Sergiovanni, T. J., 26, 29

Sheckley, B., 120, 125

Sikh community, 74

Simon, H. A., 107, 108, 113

Sirotnik, K. A., 37, 39

Site-based management, and systemic design, 89–90, 95

Sitkin, S., 26, 28

Sloan, E. S., 41, 43, 48, 51, 55

Smylie, M. A., 52, 55

Soder, R., 37, 39

Stability, in partnerships, 9

Stacey, R., 7, 14

Stamps, J., 3, 4, 6, 14

Starratt, R. J., 24, 29

States, parent involvement in, 19

Stepping Stones, 79

Stevens-Arroyo, A. M., 76, 83

Sugar Hill Gang, 69

Systemic Design Collaborative, 86–98

Tanner, D., 72, 83

Tanner, L., 72, 83

Taoism, 74

Teacher: cultures of, 60, 63; in systemic design, 87, 94–97

Teams: with health and human services

professionals, 49; for systemic design, 87–98
Teitel, L., 118, 126
Tennessee, Scopes v., 72–73
The Woodlawn Organization (TWO), 76–77
Tracy, J. R., 19, 29
Transaction costs, and contracts, 108–109
Trist, E. L., 47, 55
Trust, in partnerships, 5, 9, 87–89
Tullock, G., 101, 112
Tyack, D., 42, 55, 72, 83

U.S. Department of Education, 100, 113
United Way, 23

Value, added by partnerships, 12
Values, and religious organizations, 74–76
Vandergrift, J. A., 19, 29
Vision, for higher education institutions, 38

Washington, University of, Training for Interprofessional Collaboration at, 34

Waszak, C., 42–43, 55
Wayne State University, and charter school, 32
Wheatley, M., 116, 126
Whitmore, J., 76, 82
Williams, D. L., Jr., 24, 25, 28
Williamson, O. E., 106, 108, 113
Wise, A., 58, 70
Woodlawn Organization, The, 76–77
Worley, C. G., 42, 54
Writers: aspects of partnerships with, 57–70; assumptions of, 61; conclusion on, 69; culture of, 60, 63; and emergent leaders, 116–117; expectations for, 62–63; and knowledge integration, 66–69; lessons from program with, 64–66; relationship with, 63–64; study of, 59–60; views of, 60–62
Writers in the Schools (WITS), 59

Yale-New Haven Hospital, 33
Yale-New Haven Teachers Institute, 33
Youth for Christ, 76

Ziegler, E., 22, 118
Zigler, E. F., 42, 55